NARRATIVE OF THE LIFE OF FREDERICK DOUGLASS, AN AMERICAN SLAVE

D1302929

AN ADAPTED CLASSIC

NARRATIVE OF THE LIFE OF FREDERICK DOUGLASS, AN AMERICAN SLAVE

Written by Himself

GLOBE FEARON
EDUCATIONAL PUBLISHER

PARAMUS, NEW JERSEY

Paramount Publishing

Executive Editor: Barbara Levadi
Adapter: Prescott Hill
Senior Editor: Bernice Golden
Assistant Editor: Roger Weisman
Art Director: Nancy Sharkey
Cover and Interior Illustrations: Laurie Harden
Production Editor: Linda Greenberg
Electronic Systems Specialist: José López
Marketing Manager: Sandra Hutchison

ISBN: 0-835-91118-7

Printed in the United States of America
1 2 3 4 5 6 7 8 9 10 99 98 97 96 95 94

GLOBE FEARON
EDUCATIONAL PUBLISHER
PARAMUS, NEW JERSEY

Paramount Publishing

CONTENTS

ABOUT THE AUTHOR

Frederick Douglass was born a slave on a plantation in Maryland. His mother, Harriet Bailey, named him Frederick Augustus Washington Bailey. The exact date of his birth is not known, but historians believe it was in February 1818.

Douglass told the story of his early years in his autobiography, *Narrative of the Life of Frederick Douglass, an American Slave.*

There had been other narratives by escaped slaves before Douglass's work. His was so beautifully written that it became the classic account of the life of an American slave.

Douglass escaped from slavery in 1838. In the narrative, he does not give the details of his escape. He had two reasons for omitting these:

First, he did not want to endanger any of the people who helped him. Helping a slave to escape was a crime in the South. Some of the people who helped him still lived there.

Second, he did not want slaveholders to know the methods he used. He thought that such knowledge would help slaveholders stop other slaves from escaping.

In fact, Douglass escaped by disguising himself as a sailor. Carrying false identification papers, he took a train to Delaware. There he got on a steamboat to Philadelphia. Then he went by train and ferryboat to New York City. Soon after that, he moved to New Bedford, Massachusetts. He changed his name in order to make it more difficult for slave kidnappers to return him to slavery.

In 1841, he began to lecture to audiences about his life as a slave. The account of his life given in

Narrative of the Life of Frederick Douglass ends when he stands up before an anti-slavery audience in Nantucket, Rhode Island. He finds he can speak with ease about the evils of slavery. That moment marked the beginning of a brilliant new career.

As a result of that speech in Nantucket, the Massachusetts Anti-Slavery Society hired him. Now, he spoke before audiences throughout the North.

He was such a powerful speaker that some people questioned whether he really had been a slave. To counter those people, he wrote his autobiography. In the narrative, he gave details of his life as a slave. He included his slave name and the name of his owner.

By doing so, he placed himself in danger of being kidnapped and taken back to the South. Slave hunters at that time made a good living by kidnapping fugitive slaves. The hunters then returned the slaves to their owners in the South. Once back in bondage, the slave would be severely punished. Often the slave was sent to work on a plantation in the deep South.

To avoid such a fate, Douglass left the United States and began a speaking tour of England, Scotland, and Ireland. He spoke before huge audiences. He called for justice for all oppressed peoples regardless of their race. In England, supporters helped him raise the money to buy his freedom from his owner.

As a free man, Douglass continued to speak out against slavery. He also started his own newspaper, the *North Star*. He published it in Rochester, New York, from 1847 to 1860.

During the Civil War (1860–1865), he served as a consultant to President Abraham Lincoln. He helped recruit African Americans to fight for the North. Among the recruits were his two sons.

After the war, Douglass continued to fight for the rights of African Americans. He also spoke out against injustice of all kinds. He was a strong supporter of the women's rights movement

He continued his public service. In 1871, he became assistant secretary of the Santo Domingo Commission. From 1877 to 1888, he was a marshal in the District of Columbia. He served as United States minister to Haiti from 1889 to 1891.

Douglass died in 1895 in Washington, D.C. A true American hero, he rose from slave to respected leader. His memory will live on as long as men and women prize freedom.

ADAPTER'S NOTE

In preparing this edition of the *Narrative of the Life of Frederick Douglass*, we have retained most of what Douglass wrote and kept his main purpose in mind. We have shortened and simplified some of Douglass's sentences and paragraphs. Certain words and expressions have been retained to keep the flavor of the time period during which the book was written.

INTRODUCTION

The slavery system in the United States took many forms. The kind of slavery practiced on plantations was different from that practiced in cities. Frederick Douglass himself had experience in both the country and the city systems. This experience adds to the value of his autobiography.

The most common image of American slaves—as described in books and depicted in motion pictures—is that of the plantation slave. Such slaves worked on large farms for a single owner.

However, that presents only part of the picture. Many slaves did not work directly for their owners. A common practice was to "hire out" slaves to someone else.

For example, a slave owner might have more than enough slaves to do the work on his own plantation. He could then "hire out" surplus slaves to people who could not afford their own slaves. In a sense, they would be "renting" the slaves from the slaves' actual owner. Slaves could be rented by the day or for a longer period. One-year contracts were common.

There was an advantage to slave owners in "hiring out" their slaves on long contracts. They did not have to pay for feeding, clothing, and housing the slaves during that period. In addition, of course, the owners received money from the person who "hired" the slave.

There was also an advantage to the people who hired the slaves. They got the use of the slaves' labor only when they needed labor. They had the upkeep of the slaves only when the slaves were working for them.

What advantages did the hiring-out system offer the slaves themselves? The slavery system did not take that into account. Slaves were not considered human beings. They were considered items of property. Their feelings were not important to the slavery system.

However, a special form of hiring out developed that often was to the slave's advantage. That was the practice of "hiring one's own time." Under it, slaves would find work on their own. They would agree on payment with the person hiring them. The slave would then give part of their pay to their masters while keeping the rest.

Douglass made such an arrangement. At the end of the week, he would receive pay. Then he would turn over an agreed-upon portion to his owner, Hugh Auld.

As Douglass notes in his book, "hiring one's own time" was an unfair system. But the practice gave slaves more freedom than they had when working directly for their owners. Many—Douglass included—lived away from their owners' homes. Often, the owners didn't even know where, or for whom, their slaves were working.

Such a practice was against the law. Slave owners feared that if slaves got too much independence, they would not be happy. They would want total freedom. Of course, this was true. As a result, we have this eloquent and moving document, *Narrative of the Life of Frederick Douglass, an American Slave*.

PEOPLE AND PLACES IN THE LIFE OF FREDERICK DOUGLASS

FREDERICK DOUGLASS
The author, a former slave

HARRIET BAILEY
Frederick Douglass's mother

COLONEL EDWARD LLOYD
A rich slave holder

CAPTAIN ANTHONY
Douglass's first master

MR. PLUMMER
An overseer who worked for Captain Anthony

AUNT HESTER
Douglass's aunt

RICHARD ANTHONY
One of Captain Anthony's sons

ANDREW ANTHONY
One of Captain Anthony's sons

LUCRETIA AULD
Captain Anthony's daughter

THOMAS AULD
Douglass's second master, Lucretia's husband

HUGH AULD
Thomas Auld's brother

SOPHIA AULD
Hugh Auld's wife

LITTLE THOMAS
Hugh and Sophie Auld's son

OLD BARNEY
A slave

DEMBY
A slave

AUSTIN GORE
An overseer who killed Demby

MR. EDWARD COVEY
A "slave breaker"

MR. FREELAND
A farmer to whom Douglass was "hired out"

BALTIMORE
A city in Maryland where the Hugh Auld family lived

TALBOT COUNTY
A Maryland county on the eastern shore of Chesapeake Bay

EASTON
The town in Talbot County where Douglass was jailed

ST. MICHAEL'S
The town in Talbot County where Thomas Auld's family lived

NEW BEDFORD
The Massachusetts city where Douglass settled

Chapter 1 Born a Slave

I was born in Tuckahoe, about 12 miles from Easton, in Talbot County, Maryland. I have no knowledge of my age because I never saw any authentic[1] record containing it.

Most slaves know as little of their ages as horses know of theirs. Masters often wish to keep their slaves ignorant of such knowledge. I do not remember ever having met a slave who could tell of his birthday. Slaves seldom come nearer to it than summer, winter, spring, or fall.

Not knowing about my birthday was a source of unhappiness to me, even when I was a child. The white children all knew when they were born. I did not. I could not understand why I was not allowed to have the same privilege. I was not even allowed to ask.

My master did not think it right for slaves to ask such questions. He thought it showed they did not respect their owners. In his mind, it also showed that the slaves were restless.

The nearest estimate I can give makes me now between 27 and 28 years old. I think so because in the year 1835 I heard my master say I was about 17 years old.

My mother was named Harriet Bailey. She was the daughter of Isaac and Betsey Bailey, who were both colored and quite dark. My mother was darker than either her mother or her father.

---

1. **authentic** reliable; true

My father was a white man. He was admitted to be such by everybody I ever heard speak about my parents. I have also heard people whisper the opinion that my master was my father. I do not know if that was correct. The means of knowing the truth was withheld from me.

My mother and I were separated when I was just a baby. This is a common custom in the part of Maryland from which I ran away. Slave children are often separated from their mothers at a very early age.

Often, before the child is a year old, its mother is sent away to some farm a long distance off. The child is then placed under the care of an old woman who is too old to do the hard labor in the fields.

I do not know why mothers are separated from their children. Maybe it is so the child will not grow to love its mother and the mother to love her child. That is what happens, anyway.

I never saw my mother more than four or five times in my life. Each of those times was very short and at night. She worked on a farm owned by a Mr. Stewart, who lived about 12 miles from my home. She made her trips to see me after work, coming the whole way by foot. She worked as a field hand. A whipping is the penalty for not being in the field at sunrise.

I do not ever remember seeing my mother by the light of day. She would lie down with me at night until I fell asleep. Long before I woke up, she would be gone.

Death soon ended what little closeness we had. I was about seven when she died. I was not allowed to be present at her death or burial. She was gone long before I knew anything about it. I had never enjoyed, to any considerable extent, her soothing presence or her tender watchful care. I received the news of her death with much the same emotions I would have felt at the death of a stranger.

Called suddenly away, she left me without the slightest idea of who my father was. The whisper that my master, Captain Anthony, was my father may or may not be true. True or false, it is of but little consequence to my purpose.

The fact remains that the children of slave women follow the conditions of their mothers, not their fathers. This is true—in all its glaring evil—under the laws established by the white slaveholders. The slaveholder, in many cases, has the double relationship of master and father of his young slaves.

Such slaves always suffer greater hardships and have to put up with more than others. They are a constant annoyance to the slaveholder's wife. She is ever ready to find fault with them. She is never better pleased than when she sees them under the lash. This is true especially when she suspects her husband of showing them favors which he withholds from his other slaves.

The white master often sells the slaves he has fathered because of his wife's bad feelings about them. Cruel as the deed may strike anyone—for a man to sell his own children—it is often the kindest thing for the slaves.

Captain Anthony was my first master. He was not rich. He owned only two or three farms and about 30 slaves. His farms and slaves were under the care of an overseer named Plummer.

Mr. Plummer was a miserable drunkard, a profane[2] swearer, a savage monster. He always went armed with a whip, called a cowskin, and a heavy club. I have known him to cut and slash the women's heads so horribly that even Master would be enraged at his cruelty.

Captain Anthony, however, was not himself a

---

2. profane irreverent

humane slaveholder. He was a cruel man, hardened by a long life of slaveholding. He would at times seem to take great pleasure in whipping a slave. I have often been awakened at the dawn of day by the most heart-rending shrieks of an aunt of mine, whom he would tie up and whip.

No words, no tears, no prayers from his bloody victim seemed to move his iron heart from its purpose. The louder she screamed, the harder he whipped. Where the blood ran fastest, there he whipped longest.

I remember the first time I ever witnessed this horrible scene. I was a small child, but I never shall forget it so long as I remember anything. It struck me with awful force. It was the bloodstained gate, the entrance to the hell of slavery, through which I was about to pass.

Aunt Hester went out one night, for what I do not know. She was absent when my master wanted to see her. He had ordered her not to go out evenings. Also, he told her that she must never let him catch her with Ned Roberts. Roberts was a young slave belonging to Colonel Lloyd.

You may guess why Captain Anthony was so careful of her. She was a woman of noble form and great beauty. She had very few equals in personal appearance among the colored or white women of our neighborhood.

Aunt Hester had not only disobeyed his orders in going out. She also had been found in company with Ned Roberts.

Had Master been a man of pure morals himself, he might have been interested in protecting the innocence of my aunt. But those who knew him will not suspect him of any such virtue.

Before he began to whip Aunt Hester, he took her

into the kitchen. He stripped her from neck to waist. Her neck, shoulders, and back were left entirely naked. He then cursed her and told her to cross her hands.

He made her get upon a stool and tied her hands to a hook in the ceiling. Her arms were stretched up at their full length so that she stood upon the ends of her toes. He then said to her, "Now, I'll learn you not to disobey my orders!"

He rolled up his sleeves and began to whip her. Soon the warm, red blood began to drip onto the floor. The louder heart-rending shrieks came from her, the more horrid oaths came from him.

I was terrified and horror-stricken at the sight. I hid myself in a closet and dared not venture out till long after the whipping was over. I had never seen anything like it before. I had always lived with my grandmother on the outskirts of the plantation. I had therefore been, until now, out of the way of the bloody scenes that often occurred on the plantation.

Chapter 2 The Great House Farm

Captain Anthony's family consisted of two sons, Andrew and Richard; one daughter, Lucretia; and her husband, Captain Thomas Auld. They lived in one house, upon the home plantation of Colonel Edward Lloyd. Captain Anthony was Colonel Lloyd's clerk and superintendent. He was what might be called the overseer of the overseers.

I spent two years of my childhood on this plantation in Captain Anthony's family. It was here that I witnessed the bloody act recorded in the first chapter. I received my first impressions of slavery on this plantation. I will give some description of it and of slavery as it existed there.

The plantation is about 12 miles north of Easton, in Talbot County, on the eastern shore of Chesapeake Bay. The main products raised upon it were tobacco, corn, and wheat. These were raised in great abundance. My master constantly used a large sloop to carry crops to market in Baltimore. With these products and the products from his other farms, he was able to keep the sloop in constant use.

Colonel Lloyd kept from 300 to 400 slaves on his home plantation. He owned a large number more on the 20 or so neighboring farms belonging to him.

The home plantation was the great business place. It was the seat of government for all the farms. All disputes among the overseers of any of the farms were settled here. If a slave was convicted of a serious crime, became unmanageable, or tried to run away, he was brought immediately here. Then he would be severely whipped, put on board the sloop, carried to Baltimore, and sold to a slave trader as a warning to the slaves remaining.

Here, too, the slaves of all the other farms received their monthly allowance of food and their yearly clothing allowance. Each month the men and women slaves received eight pounds of pork, or its equivalent in fish, and one bushel of cornmeal.

Their yearly clothing allowance consisted of two coarse linen shirts, one pair of linen trousers, one jacket, one pair of heavy trousers for winter, one pair of stockings, and one pair of shoes. All this could not have cost more than seven dollars.

The allowance of the slave children was given to their mothers or the old women having the care of them. The children unable to work in the field had neither shoes, stockings, jackets, nor trousers given to them. Their clothing consisted of two coarse linen shirts per year. When these failed them, they went naked until the next allowance day. Children from seven to ten years old, of both sexes, almost naked, might be seen at all seasons of the year.

The slaves had no beds, unless one coarse blanket can be considered such, and none but the men and women had these. This, however, is not considered the greatest hardship. For it is less difficult to be without a bed than without the time to sleep. When their day's work in the field is done, most slaves have their washing, mending, and cooking to do. They have few or none of the ordinary tools for doing these tasks. So very many of their sleeping hours are taken up doing them. When they are finally done, old and young, male and female, married and single, drop down side by side, on one common bed—the cold, damp floor. They cover themselves with their miserable blankets. Here they sleep till they are called to the field by the driver's horn.

At the sound of the horn, all must rise, and be off to the field. There must be no stopping. Everyone must be at his or her post. Mr. Severe, the overseer, would stand by the door of the quarter, armed with a large hickory stick and heavy cowskin. He would be ready to whip anyone who was not ready to start at the sound of the horn.

Mr. Severe was rightly named: he was a cruel man. I have seen him whip a woman, causing the blood to run half an hour at a time. He did this while her crying children pleaded for their mother's release. He seemed to take pleasure in such acts. Added to his cruelty, he was a profane swearer. It was enough to chill the blood and stiffen the hair of an ordinary man to hear him talk.

From the rising till the going down of the sun, he was cursing, raving, cutting, and slashing among the slaves of the field in the most frightful manner.

He died very soon after I went to Colonel Lloyd's. He died as he lived—uttering, with his dying groans, bitter curses and horrid oaths.

Mr. Severe's place was filled by a Mr. Hopkins. He was a very different man. He was less cruel and less profane than Mr. Severe. He whipped but seemed to take no pleasure in it. He was called by the slaves a good overseer.

The home plantation of Colonel Lloyd had the appearance of a country village. All the mechanical operations for all the farms were performed here. The shoemaking and mending, the blacksmithing, weaving, and grain-grinding were all performed by the slaves on the home plantation.

The whole place had a businesslike appearance, which was very unlike the neighboring farms. The number of houses, too, gave it an advantage over the neighboring farms. It was called by the slaves the *Great House Farm*. Few privileges were considered higher by the slaves of the out-farms than that of being selected to do errands at the Great House

The slaves selected to go to the Great House Farm were strangely enthusiastic. Perhaps it was the monthly allowance for themselves and their fellow slaves. While on their way, they would make the dense old woods for miles around vibrate with their wild songs. These songs revealed at once the highest joy and the deepest sadness.

They would sometimes sing the saddest words in the happiest tone and the happiest words in the most pathetic tone. Into all of their songs they would manage to weave in something of the Great House Farm, such as the following words:

"I am going away to the Great House Farm!

O, yea! O, yea! O!"

The words were full of meaning to them. They told a tale of woe. The tones were loud, long, and deep. They breathed the prayer and complaint of souls boiling over with the bitterest anguish. Every tone cried out against slavery and a prayer to God for deliverance from chains.

Hearing those songs always depressed my spirit and filled me with sadness. I have frequently found myself in tears while hearing them. Just thinking of those sounds, even now, afflicts me. While I am writing these lines, an expression of feeling has already found its way down my cheek.

To those songs, I trace my first ideas of the dehumanizing[1] character of slavery. I can never get rid of those ideas. Those songs still follow me to deepen my hatred of slavery. If anyone wishes to be impressed with the soul-killing effects of slavery, let him go to Colonel Lloyd's plantation on allowance day. He should place himself in the deep pine woods. There, in silence, let him take in the sounds that pass through the chambers of his soul.

I have often been astonished, since I came to the North, to find people who say the slaves' singing is evidence of their contentment and happiness. It is impossible to conceive of a greater mistake.

Slaves sing most when they are most unhappy. The songs of the slave represent the sorrows of his heart. He is relieved by them, only as an aching heart is relieved by its tears. At least, such is my experience. I have often sung to drown my sorrow, but seldom to express my happiness. Crying for joy and singing for joy were both uncommon to me while in the jaws of slavery.

---

1. dehumanizing depriving of human qualities; making someone like an animal or a machine

Chapter 3 A Slave's Life

Colonel Lloyd kept a large and well-cultivated garden which gave almost constant employment to four slaves. This garden was probably the greatest attraction of the place.

During the summer, people came from far and near—from Baltimore, Easton, and Annapolis—to see it. It had fruits of almost every description, from the hardy apple of the north to the delicate orange of the south. This garden was a source of trouble on the plantation. Its excellent fruit was a strong temptation to the hungry swarms of boys as well as to the older slaves belonging to Colonel Lloyd.

Scarcely a day passed during the summer but that some slave was lashed for stealing fruit. The colonel had to resort to all kinds of plans to keep his slaves out of the garden.

The last and most successful one was that of tarring his fence all around. After that, if a slave was caught with any tar upon his person, it was deemed proof that he had either been into the garden or had tried to get in. In either case, he was severely whipped by the chief gardener. This plan worked well. The slaves became as fearful of tar as of the lash.

The colonel also kept excellent horses and carriages. His stable and carriage house presented the appearance of some of our large city establishments. His horses were of the finest form and noblest blood. His carriage house contained three splendid coaches and a half dozen or so other carriages of various sizes.

This establishment was under the care of two slaves—old Barney and young Barney—father and son. To attend to this establishment was their sole work. But it was by no means an easy employment. In nothing was Colonel Lloyd more particular than in the management of his horses.

He considered the slightest inattention to the horses to be unpardonable.[1] It brought to those under whose care they were placed the severest punishment. No excuse could shield them. That made the jobs of old and young Barney very trying ones. They never knew when they were safe from punishment. They were frequently whipped when least deserving and escaped whipping when most deserving it. Everything depended upon the looks of the horses and the state of Colonel Lloyd's mind when his horses were brought to him.

If a horse did not move fast enough or hold his head high enough, it was because of some fault of his keepers. It was painful to stand near the stable door and hear the various complaints against the keepers when a horse was taken out. "This horse has not had proper attention. He has not been sufficiently rubbed and curried. He has not been properly fed. His food was too wet or too dry. He got it too soon or too late. He was too hot or too cold. He had too much hay and not enough grain. He had too much grain and not enough hay. Old Barney did not attend to this horse. He very improperly left it to his son."

To all these complaints, no matter how unjust, the slave must never answer a word. Colonel Lloyd could not put up with any contradiction[2] from a slave. When

---

1. **unpardonable** unforgivable
2. **contradiction** a denial; a statement in opposition to another

he spoke, a slave must stand, listen, and tremble. I have seen Colonel Lloyd make old Barney, a man between 50 and 60 years of age, uncover his bald head. He then knelt down upon the cold, damp ground and received upon his toil-worn shoulders more than 30 lashes at a time.

Colonel Lloyd had three sons—Edward, Murray, and Daniel—and three sons-in-law, Mr. Winder, Mr. Nicholson, and Mr. Lowndes. They all lived at the Great House Farm and enjoyed the luxury of whipping the servants whenever they pleased.

I have seen Winder make one of the house servants stand far enough away to be touched with the end of his whip. At every stroke, Winder raised great ridges upon the servant's back.

To describe the wealth of Colonel Lloyd would be almost equal to describing the riches of Job.[3] He kept from ten to fifteen house servants. He was said to own a thousand slaves, and I think this estimate quite within the truth. Colonel Lloyd owned so many that he did not know them when he saw them. Nor did all the slaves of the out-farms know him.

It is reported that while riding along the road one day, he met a colored man. Colonel Lloyd addressed him in the usual manner of speaking to colored people on the public highways of the South. "Well, boy, whom do you belong to?"

"To Colonel Lloyd," replied the slave.

"Well, does the colonel treat you well?"

"No, sir," was the ready reply.

"What, does he work you too hard?"

"Yes, sir."

"Well, doesn't he give you enough to eat?"

---

3. Job a hero from the Bible who loses everything and endures suffering with strength and faith

"Yes, sir, he gives me enough, such as it is."

The colonel, after learning where the slave belonged, rode on. The man also went on about his business, not dreaming that he had been conversing with his master. He thought, said, and heard nothing more of the matter until two or three weeks afterwards. The poor man was then informed by his overseer that, for having found fault with his master, he was now to be sold to a Georgia slave-trader.

He was immediately chained and handcuffed. Without a moment's warning, he was snatched away. He was forever separated from his family and friends. This is the penalty for telling the truth, for telling the simple truth in answer to a series of plain questions.

It is partly because of such incidents that slaves, when asked of their condition and the character of their masters, almost always say they are contented, and that their masters are kind.

The slaveholders have been known to send in spies among their slaves. These spies are to learn their views and feelings in regard to their condition. The frequency of this has led to the saying among the slaves that a still tongue makes a wise head. They suppress the truth rather than take the consequences of telling it.

If they have anything to say of their masters, it is generally in their masters' favor. This is so especially when speaking to someone they don't know well.

I had been frequently asked—when a slave—if I had a kind master. I do not remember ever to have given a negative answer. I did not, in doing so, consider myself as saying what was absolutely false. For I always measured the kindness of my master by the standard of kindness set up among slaveholders around us.

Slaves are like other people. They think their own things better than those of others. Many think their own masters are better than the masters of other slaves. This, too, is thought in some cases when the very reverse is true.

Indeed, it is not uncommon for slaves even to quarrel among themselves about the relative goodness of their masters. Each argues for the superior goodness of his own over that of the others. But those same slaves would speak against their masters when they weren't making comparisons.

It was so on our plantation. When Colonel Lloyd's slaves met the slaves of Jacob Jepson, they seldom parted without a quarrel about their masters. Colonel Lloyd's slaves would say he was the richest. Mr. Jepson's slaves argued that he was the smartest. Colonel Lloyd's slaves would boast about his ability to buy and sell Jacob Jepson. Mr. Jepson's slaves would boast about his ability to whip Colonel Lloyd.

These quarrels would almost always end in a fight between the slaves. They seemed to think that the greatness of their masters transferred to themselves. It was bad enough to be a slave. But to be a poor man's slave was considered a disgrace indeed!

Chapter 4 Murder Goes Unpunished

Mr. Hopkins remained but a short time in the office of overseer. Why his career was so short, I do not know. I suppose he lacked the necessary severity to suit Colonel Lloyd. He was succeeded by Mr. Austin Gore.

Mr. Gore had served Colonel Lloyd as an overseer on one of the out-farms. He had shown himself worthy of the high station of overseer at the Great House Farm.

Mr. Gore was proud, ambitious, crafty, cruel, and hard-hearted. He was just the man for such a place, and it was just the place for such a man. It provided a wide area for the full exercise of all his powers. He seemed to be perfectly at home in it.

He was one of those who could twist a slave's slightest look, word, or gesture into impudence,[1] and would punish it accordingly. Answering back to him was not allowed. A slave was not allowed to claim that he had been wrongfully accused. Mr. Gore acted fully up to the rule laid down by slaveholders: "It is better that a dozen slaves suffer under the lash than that the overseer should be convicted, in the presence of the slaves, of having been at fault."

No matter how innocent a slave might be, it didn't help when accused by Mr. Gore of anything. To be accused was to be convicted, and to be convicted was to be punished.

He was cruel enough to inflict the severest punish-

---

1. **impudence** rudeness, lack of respect

ment. He was crafty enough to descend to the lowest trickery. He was hard-hearted enough to ignore the voice of a conscience. He was, of all the overseers, the most dreaded by the slaves. His presence was painful. Seldom was his sharp, shrill voice heard without producing horror and trembling in their ranks.

Mr. Gore was a serious man. Though he was a young man, he told no jokes, said no funny words, and seldom smiled. His words were in perfect keeping with his looks, and his looks were in perfect keeping with his words. Overseers will sometimes indulge in a witty word, even with the slaves. Not so with Mr. Gore. He spoke only to command and commanded only to be obeyed. He never used words when a whipping would answer as well.

When he whipped, he seemed to do so from a sense of duty and feared no consequences. He did nothing reluctantly, no matter how disagreeable. He never promised something without doing it. He was, in a word, a man of the most inflexible firmness and stone-like coolness. His savagery was equaled only by the coolness with which he committed the grossest and most savage deeds upon the slaves under his charge.

Mr. Gore once undertook to whip one of Colonel Lloyd's slaves by the name of Demby. After a few lashes, Demby ran and plunged himself into a creek. He stood there at the depth of his shoulders, refusing to come out. Mr. Gore told him that he would give him three calls. If he did not come out at the third call, Mr. Gore would shoot him.

The first call was given. Demby made no response and stood his ground. The second and third calls were given with the same result. Mr. Gore then raised his musket to Demby's face, taking deadly aim at his standing victim. In an instant, poor Demby was no more. His mangled body sank out of sight, and blood and brains marked the water where he had stood.

Horror flashed through every soul upon the plantation, excepting Mr. Gore. He alone seemed cool and collected. He was asked by Colonel Lloyd why he took such an action. His reply was that Demby had become unmanageable. He was setting a dangerous example for the other slaves. If allowed to pass without some demonstration on his part, it would finally lead to the total undermining of all rule and order upon the plantation.

He argued that if one slave refused to be corrected—and escaped with his life—the other slaves would soon copy the example. The result would be the freedom of the slaves and the enslavement of the whites.

Mr. Gore's defense was satisfactory. He was continued in his station as overseer upon the home plantation. His fame as an overseer went abroad. His horrid crime was not even investigated. It was committed in the presence of slaves. They, of course, could neither bring suit nor testify against him. Thus, a man guilty of one of the bloodiest and most foul murders went unpunished.

Mr. Gore lived in St. Michael's, Talbot County, Maryland, when I left there. If he is still alive, he very probably lives there now. If so, he is now, as he was then, highly respected, as though his guilty soul had not been stained with his brother's blood.

Killing a slave, or any colored person, in Talbot County, Maryland, is not treated as a crime, either by the courts or the community.

Mr. Thomas Lanman, of St. Michael's, killed two slaves. One of them he killed with a hatchet by knocking his brains out. He used to boast of the awful and bloody deed. I have heard him do so laughingly. He said, among other things, that when others would do as much as he had done, we should be relieved of "the niggers."

The wife of Mr. Giles Hicks, living but a short distance from where I used to live, murdered my wife's cousin. She was a young girl between 15 and 16 years of age. Mrs. Hicks mangled her body in the most horrible manner. She broke my cousin's nose and breastbone with a stick so that the poor girl died a few hours afterward.

She was immediately buried. She had not been in her grave more than a few hours before she was taken up and examined by the coroner. He decided that she had come to her death by severe beating.

The offense for which this girl was murdered was this. She had been assigned that night to mind Mrs. Hicks's baby. During the night she fell asleep, and the baby cried. Having lost her rest for several nights previous, she did not hear the crying. They were both in the room with Mrs. Hicks. Mrs. Hicks, finding the girl slow to move, jumped from her bed. She seized an oak stick of wood by the fireplace and with it broke the girl's nose and breastbone and thus ended her life.

I will not say that this most horrid murder produced no sensation in the community. It did produce sensation, but not enough to bring the murderess to punishment. There was a warrant issued for her arrest, but it was never served. Thus she escaped not only punishment, but even the pain of being tried before a court for her horrid crime.

While I am detailing bloody deeds which took place during my stay on Colonel Lloyd's plantation, I will briefly narrate another. This act occurred about the same time as the murder of Demby by Mr. Gore.

Colonel Lloyd's slaves were in the habit of spending

a part of their nights and Sundays in fishing for oysters. An old man belonging to Colonel Lloyd happened to go beyond the limits of Colonel Lloyd's property, and onto the premises of Mr. Beal Bondly. Mr. Bondly took offense. With his musket, he came down to the shore and blew its deadly contents into the poor old man.

Mr. Bondly came over to see Colonel Lloyd the next day, whether to pay him for his property, or to justify himself in what he had done, I do not know. At any rate, this whole fiendish[2] action was soon hushed up. There was very little said about it at all, and nothing done. It was a common saying, even among little white boys, that it was worth a half cent to kill a "nigger" and a half cent to bury one.

---

2. **fiendish** inhuman

Chapter 5 Leaving the Plantation

As to my own treatment while I lived on Colonel Lloyd's plantation, it was very similar to that of the other slave children. I was not old enough to work in the field. There being little else than field work to do, I had a great deal of leisure time.

The most I had to do was to drive home the cows at evening and keep the chickens out of the garden. I also had to keep the front yard clean and run errands for my old master's daughter, Mrs. Lucretia Auld.

Most of my leisure time I spent in helping Master Daniel Lloyd in finding his birds after he had shot them. My connection with Master Daniel was of some advantage to me. He became quite attached to me and was a sort of protector of me. He would not allow the older boys to pick on me and would divide his cakes with me.

I was seldom whipped by my old master. I suffered little from anything other than hunger and cold. In hottest summer and coldest winter, I was kept almost naked. I had no shoes, no stockings, no jacket, and no trousers. I had nothing on but a coarse linen shirt, reaching only to my knees.

I had no bed. I would have perished[1] with cold. But on the coldest nights, I used to steal a bag which was used for carrying corn to the mill. I would crawl into this bag. Then I would sleep there on the cold, damp, clay floor, with my head in and feet out. My feet have

---

1. **perished** died

been so cracked with the frost that the pen with which I am writing might be laid in the gashes.

We children were not given a regular allowance of food. Our food was coarse boiled cornmeal. This was called mush. It was put into a large wooden tray or trough and set down upon the ground. The children were then called, like so many pigs, and like so many pigs they would come and devour the mush. Some ate with oyster shells, others with pieces of shingle, some with naked hands, and none with spoons.

He that ate fastest got most. He that was strongest secured the best place. Few left the trough satisfied.

I was probably between seven and eight years old when I left Colonel Lloyd's plantation. I left it with joy. I shall never forget the ecstasy with which I received the news that Captain Anthony had decided to let me go to Baltimore. I was to live with Mr. Hugh Auld, brother of Captain Anthony's son-in-law, Captain Thomas Auld.

I received this information about three days before I was to go. They were three of the happiest days I ever enjoyed. I spent the most part of those three days in the creek. I washed off the plantation dirt and prepared myself for my departure.

I spent the time in washing, not so much because I wished to. Mrs. Lucretia had told me I must get all the dead skin off my feet and knees before I could go to Baltimore. She said the people in Baltimore were very clean. They would laugh at me if I looked dirty. Besides, she was going to give me a pair of trousers, and I could not put them on until I got all the dirt off me.

The thought of owning a pair of trousers was great indeed! It was almost a sufficient motive, not only to make me take off what would be called the mange by pig farmers, but the skin itself. I went at it in good earnest, working for the first time in my life with the hope of reward.

The ties that ordinarily bind children to their homes were all suspended in my case. I found no trouble in my departure. My home was charmless. It was not home to me. Upon parting from it, I could not feel that I was leaving anything which I could have enjoyed by staying. My mother was dead. My grandmother lived far off, and I seldom saw her. I had two sisters and one brother who lived in the same house with me. The early separation of us from our mother had just about blotted out the relationship from our memories.

I looked for home elsewhere. I was confident that I would not find one which I should like less than the one I was leaving. If, however, I found in my new home hardship, hunger, whipping, and nakedness, I had the consolation that I should not have escaped any one of them by staying.

I had the strongest desire to see Baltimore. My cousin Tom, though not fluent in speech, had inspired me with that desire by his description of the place. I could never point out anything at the Great House, no matter how beautiful or powerful, but that he had seen something at Baltimore far exceeding it, both in beauty and in strength.

I left the Great House Farm without a regret and with the highest hopes of future happiness.

We sailed for Baltimore on a Saturday morning. I remember only the day of the week. At that time I had no knowledge of the days of the month nor the months of the year. On setting sail, I walked to the rear of the sloop and gave to Colonel Lloyd's plantation what I hoped would be the last look. I then placed myself in the bow of the sloop. There I spent the remainder of the day thinking about what lay ahead of me rather than in things nearby or behind.

In the afternoon of that day, we reached Annapolis, the capital of the state. We stopped but a few moments, so that I had no time to go on shore. It was the first large town that I had ever seen. Though it would look small compared with some of our New England factory villages, I thought it a wonderful place for its size.

We arrived at Baltimore early on Sunday morning, landing at Smith's Wharf, not far from Bowley's Wharf. We had on board the sloop a large flock of sheep. After helping in driving them to the slaughterhouse of Mr. Curtis on Louden Slater's Hill, I was taken to my new home in Alliciana Street.

Mr. and Mrs. Auld were both at home and met me at the door with their little son, Thomas. Here I saw what I had never seen before. It was a white face beaming with the most kindly emotions—the face of my new mistress, Sophia Auld. I wish I could describe the joy that flashed through my soul as I beheld it. It was a new and strange sight to me, brightening up my pathway with the light of happiness. Little Thomas was told that I was his Freddy, and I was told to take care of little Thomas. Thus I began the duties of my new home with the most cheering prospect ahead.

I look upon my departure from Colonel Lloyd's plantation as one of the most important events of my life. It is possible that if I had not left the plantation, I should today—instead of being here seated by my own table in the enjoyment of freedom and the happiness of home, writing this Narrative—be confined in the chains of slavery.

Going to live at Baltimore laid the foundation for all

my later success. My life has been marked with so many favors that I have always believed some Providence[2] was watching over me. I regarded the selection of myself for going to Baltimore as being somewhat remarkable.

Many other slave children might have been sent from the plantation to Baltimore. There were those younger, those older, and those of the same age. I was chosen from among them all, and was the first, last, and only choice.

I may be thought superstitious, and even self-important, in regarding this event as a case of Providence acting in my favor. From my earliest recollection, I had a deep conviction that slavery would not always be able to hold me within its foul embrace. In the darkest hours of my life as a slave, this faith and spirit of hope did not leave me. It remained like a guiding angel to cheer me through the gloom. This good spirit was from God, and to him I offer thanksgiving and praise.

---

2. Providence divine guidance; God

Chapter 6 My Baltimore Home

My new mistress proved to be all she appeared when I first met her. She was a woman of the kindest heart and finest feelings. She had never had a slave under her control before me. Before she was married, she had worked for a living. She was a weaver. By staying very busy at her work, she had been kept away from the dehumanizing effects of slavery.

I was utterly astonished at her goodness. I scarcely knew how to behave toward her. She was entirely unlike any other white woman I had ever seen. I could not approach her as I was accustomed to approach other white ladies. My early instruction was all out of place.

She did not demand the servility,[1] usually so acceptable a quality in a slave. Her favor was not gained by it. In fact, she seemed to be disturbed by it. She did not think it impudent or unmannerly for a slave to look her in the face. The meanest slave was put fully at ease in her presence, and none left without feeling better for having seen her. Her face was made of heavenly smiles and her voice of tranquil music.

But, alas! This kind heart had but a short time to remain such. The fatal poison of irresponsible power was already in her hands and soon started its infernal

---

1. **servility** humbleness before others; acting like a servant

work. That cheerful eye, under the influence of slavery, soon became red with rage. That voice, made all of sweet accord, changed to one of harsh and horrid discord. That angelic face gave place to that of a demon.

Soon after I went to live with Mr. and Mrs. Auld, she very kindly started to teach me the A, B, C's. After I had learned this, she assisted me in learning to spell words of three or four letters.

Just at this point in my progress, Mr. Auld found out what was going on. At once he forbade Mrs. Auld to instruct me further. He told her, among other things, that it was unlawful as well as unsafe to teach a slave to read.

To use his own words further, he said, "If you give a nigger an inch, he will take a mile. A nigger should know nothing but to obey his master—to do as he is told to do. Learning would spoil the best nigger in the world.

"If you teach that nigger (speaking of myself) how to read, there would be no keeping him. It would forever unfit him to be a slave. He would at once become unmanageable and of no value to his master. As to himself, it could do him no good, but a great deal of harm. It would make him discontented and unhappy."

These words sank deep into my heart. They stirred up feelings that lay slumbering within and started an entirely new train of thought. It was a new and special revelation, explaining dark and mysterious things, with which my youthful understanding had struggled, in vain.

I now understood what had been to me a most perplexing difficulty: the white man's power to enslave the black man. From that moment, I understood the pathway from slavery to freedom. It was just what I wanted, and I got it at a time when I least expected it.

I was saddened by the thought of losing the aid of my kind mistress. I was gladdened, however, by the invaluable instruction which I had gained from my master. Though conscious of the difficulty of learning without a teacher, I set out with high hopes and a fixed purpose, at whatever cost of trouble, to learn how to read.

The very manner with which he tried to impress his wife with the evil consequences of giving me instruction served to convince me of the truths he was uttering. What he most dreaded, that I most desired. What he most loved, that I most hated. That which to him was a great evil was to me a great good to be sought. The argument which he so warmly urged against my learning to read only served to inspire me with a desire and determination to learn. In learning to read, I owe almost as much to the bitter opposition of my master as to the kindly aid of my mistress. I acknowledge the benefit of both.

I had lived but a short time in Baltimore before I observed a marked difference in the treatment of slaves, compared to what I had witnessed in the country. A city slave is almost a free man compared with a slave on the plantation. He is much better fed and clothed and enjoys privileges altogether unknown to the slave on the plantation. There is a shred of decency, a sense of shame, that does much to curb and check those outbreaks of terrible cruelty so common on the plantation.

It is a desperate slaveholder who will shock the humanity of his neighbors who don't hold slaves with the cries of his beaten slave. Few are willing to incur the reputation of being a cruel master.

Above all things, a city slaveholder does not want to be known as not giving a slave enough to eat. Every city slaveholder is anxious to have it known that he feeds his slaves well. Most of them do give their slaves enough to eat. There are, however, some painful exceptions to this rule.

Directly opposite to us, on Philpot Street, lived Mr. Thomas Hamilton. He owned two slaves. Their names were Henrietta and Mary. Henrietta was about 22 years of age, and Mary was about 14. Of all the beaten, skinny creatures I ever looked upon, these two were the most so. His heart must be harder than stone that could look upon these unmoved.

The head, neck, and shoulders of Mary were literally cut to pieces. I have frequently felt her head and found it nearly covered with festering sores, caused by the lash of her cruel mistress. I do not know that her master ever whipped her, but I have been an eyewitness to the cruelty of Mrs. Hamilton.

I used to be in Mr. Hamilton's house nearly every day. Mrs. Hamilton used to sit in a large chair with a heavy cowskin always by her side. Hardly an hour passed without being marked by the blood of one of these slaves.

The girls seldom passed her without her saying, "Move faster, you *black gip!*" At the same time, she gave them a blow with the cowskin over the head or shoulders, often drawing blood. She would then say, "Take that, you *black gip!*"—continuing, "If you don't move faster, I'll move you!"

Added to the crude lashings to which these slaves were subjected, they were kept nearly half-starved. They seldom knew what it was to eat a full meal. I have seen Mary competing with the pigs for the garbage thrown into the street.

Chapter 7 Learning to Read and Write

I lived with Master Hugh's family about seven years. During this time, I succeeded in learning to read and write. In doing this, I was compelled to resort to various tricks. I had no regular teacher. My mistress, who had kindly started to instruct me, had, by the advice and direction of her husband, stopped the lessons. Not only that, she tried to stop me from being instructed by anyone else.

My mistress was, as I have said, a kind and tenderhearted woman. In the simplicity of her soul, she started, when I first went to live with her, to treat me as she supposed one human being ought to treat another. But slavery proved as damaging to her as it did to me.

When I went there, she was a pious,[1] warm, and tenderhearted woman. There was no sorrow or suffering for which she had not a tear. She had bread for the hungry, clothes for the naked, and comfort for every mourner who came within her reach.

Slavery soon proved its ability to take away these heavenly qualities. Under its influence, the tender heart became stone, and the lamb-like disposition gave way to one of tiger-like fierceness. The first step in her downfall was her stopping my instruction. She finally became even more violent in her opposition than her husband himself.

She was not satisfied with simply doing as well as

---

1. **pious** religious

he had commanded. She seemed anxious to do better. Nothing seemed to make her more angry than to see me with a newspaper. She seemed to think that here lay the danger. I have had her rush at me with a face made all up of fury and snatch from me a newspaper.

But her efforts came too late. Mistress, in teaching me the alphabet, had given me the inch. No precaution could prevent me from taking the mile.

The plan I adopted, and the one by which I was most successful, was that of making friends of all the little white boys whom I met in the street. As many of these as I could, I converted into teachers. With their kindly aid, obtained at different times and in different places, I finally succeeded in learning to read.

When I was sent on errands, I always took my book with me. By doing my errands quickly, I found time to get a lesson before my return. I always used to carry bread with me, enough of which was always in the house. I was always welcome to it. I was much better off in this regard than many of the poor white children in our neighborhood. In return for this bread, the hungry little boys would give me that more valuable bread of knowledge.

I used to talk about slavery with them. I would sometimes say to them that I wished I could be as free as they would be when they got to be men.

"You will be free as soon as you are 21, but I am a slave for life! Have not I as much a right to be free as you have?"

I was now about 12 years old. The thought of being a slave for life began to bear heavily upon my heart. Just about this time, I got hold of a book entitled *The Columbian Orator*. Every opportunity I got, I used to read this book.

Among much other interesting matter, I found in it demonstrations of the power of truth. It also offered many a bold attack against slavery and many a powerful argument of human rights.

The reading of these documents enabled me to utter my thoughts and to meet the arguments brought forward in favor of slavery. But while they relieved me of one difficulty, they brought on another even more painful than the one of which I was relieved.

The more I read, the more I was led to loathe[2] my enslavers. I could regard them in no other light than as a band of robbers. They had left their homes and gone to Africa and stolen us from our homes. They reduced us to slavery in a strange land. I loathed them as being the meanest as well as the most wicked of men.

As I read and thought about the subject, behold! That very discontentment which Master Hugh had predicted would follow my learning to read had already come to torment and sting my soul.

I would at times feel that learning to read had been a curse rather than a blessing. It had given me a view of my wretched condition without the remedy. It opened my eyes to the horrible pit, but to no ladder upon which to get out.

In moments of agony, I envied my fellow slaves for their stupidity. I have often wished myself a beast. Anything, no matter what, to get rid of thinking! It was this everlasting thinking about my condition that tormented me.

But there was no getting rid of it. The silver trumpet of freedom had awakened my soul. I heard freedom in every sound and saw it in every sight.

---

2. loathe hate; detest

While in this state of mind, I was eager to hear anyone speak of slavery. I was a ready listener. Every little while, I could hear something about the *abolitionists*.[3] It was some time before I found what the word meant. It was always used in such connections as to make it an interesting word to me.

If a slave ran away and succeeded, or if a slave killed his master, set fire to a barn, or did anything very wrong in the mind of a slaveholder, it was spoken of as the results of abolition.

Hearing the word in this connection very often, I set about learning what it meant. The dictionary afforded me little or no help. I found it was "the act of abolishing"; but then I did not know what was to be abolished. Here I was puzzled. I did not dare to ask anyone about its meaning, for I was satisfied that it was something they wanted me to know very little about.

I got one of our city papers. It contained an account of a number of petitions from the North. They asked for the abolition of slavery in the District of Columbia and for an end to the slave trade between the states. From then on I understood the words *abolition* and *abolitionist*. I always drew near when those words were spoken, expecting to hear something of importance to myself and to my fellow slaves.

The light broke in upon me by degrees. I went one day down to the waterfront and saw two Irishmen unloading stones from a boat. I went, unasked, and helped them. When we had finished, one of them came to me and asked me if I were a slave. I told him I was. He asked, "Are ye a slave for life?"

---

3. abolitionists opponents of slavery; members of the movement to abolish slavery

I told him that I was. They seemed to be deeply affected by the statement. They advised me to run away to the North. I should find friends there, and I should be free.

I pretended not to be interested in what they said and treated them as if I did not understand them. White men have been known to encourage slaves to escape. Then they catch them and return them to their masters for a reward.

I was afraid that these seemingly good men might use me so. But still I remembered their advice. I felt I should one day find a good chance to run away.

Meanwhile, I would learn to write.

The idea as to how I might learn to write was suggested to me by being in Durgin and Bailey's shipyard. There I watched the ship carpenters write on a timber the name of that part of the ship for which it was intended. When a piece of timber was intended for the larboard side, it would be marked "L." When a piece was for the starboard side, it would be marked "S." A piece for the larboard side forward would be marked thus: "L.F." When a piece was for the starboard side forward, it would be marked "S.F." For larboard aft, it would be marked "L.A." For starboard aft, it would be marked "S.A."

I soon learned the names of these letters, and for what they were intended. I immediately began to copy them. In a short time, I was able to make the four letters named.

After that, when I met with any boy who I knew could write, I would tell him I could write as well as he. The next word would be, "I don't believe you. Let me see you try it."

I would then make the letters which I had been so fortunate as to learn and would ask him to beat that.

In this way, I got a good many lessons in writing, which it is quite possible I should never have gotten in any other way. My copybook was the board fence, brick wall, and pavement. My pen and ink was a lump of chalk.

By this time, my little Master Thomas had gone to school and learned how to write and had filled a number of copybooks. These had been brought home from school and then laid aside. I used to write in the spaces left in the copybooks, copying what Master Thomas had written. Thus, after a long, tedious effort for years, I finally succeeded in learning how to write.

Chapter 8 The Valuation

When I was about 10 or 11, my old master, Captain Anthony, had died. His son Richard had died earlier. That left only his son Andrew and his daughter Lucretia to share his estate.

Because he left no will, it was now necessary to value the property so it could be equally divided between Lucretia and Andrew. I was sent for, in order to be valued along with the other property.

Here again my feelings of loathing rose up against slavery. It gave me a new conception of my degraded condition.

I left Baltimore with a young heart full of sadness and a soul full of worry. After sailing about 24 hours, I found myself near the place of my birth.

We were all ranked together at the valuation.[1] Men and women, old and young, married and single, were ranked with horses, sheep, and swine.

Silvery-headed men and lively youth, maids and matrons, had to undergo the same inspection. At this moment, I saw more clearly than ever the brutalizing effects of slavery upon both slave and slaveholder.

After the valuation came the division. Words cannot express the high excitement and deep anxiety which were felt among us poor slaves during this time.

Our fate for life was now to be decided. We had no more voice in that decision than the animals

---

1. **valuation** the act of deciding the value or price of something; a gathering where that is done

among whom we were ranked. A single word from the white men was enough—against all our wishes and prayers—to separate forever the dearest friends, dearest relatives, and strongest ties known to human beings.

In addition to the pain of separation, there was the fear of falling into the hands of Master Andrew Anthony. He was known to us all as a cruel man and a common drunkard. He had already wasted a large portion of his father's wealth. We all felt that we might as well be sold at once to the Georgia slave-traders as to pass into his hands. We knew that would happen anyway, once he owned us. It was something we all held in the utmost horror and fear.

I worried more than most of my fellow slaves. I had known what it was to be treated kindly, and they had not. They had seen little or nothing of the world. They were indeed men and women of sorrow. Their backs had been made familiar with the bloody lash, so that they had become hardened.

My back was still tender, for while at Baltimore, I got few whippings. Few slaves could boast of a kinder master and mistress than mine.

The thought of passing out of their hands into those of Master Andrew was well calculated to make me anxious as to my fate. A few days before—to give me a sample of his bloody disposition—he took my little brother by the throat, threw him on the ground, and with the heel of his boot stamped upon his head till the blood gushed from his nose and ears.

Then he turned to me and said that was what he would do to me one of these days. He meant—I suppose—when he came to own me.

Thanks to a kind Providence, I went to Lucretia. She sent me immediately back to Baltimore to live again in the family of Master Hugh. It was a glad day for me. I was absent from Baltimore for just about one month, but it seemed like six months.

Very soon after my return to Baltimore, Lucretia died, survived by her husband Thomas. In a very short time after Lucretia's death, Master Andrew died.

Now all the property of my old master, slaves included, was in the hands of strangers—strangers who had had nothing to do with gathering it. Not one of us slaves was let free. We all remained slaves, from the youngest to the oldest.

Something happened then that deepened my hatred of slavery and of slaveholders. It was the treatment given to my poor old grandmother.

She had served my old master faithfully from youth to old age. She had rocked him in infancy, taken care of him in childhood, and served him through life. At his death, she wiped from his icy brow the cold death-sweat and closed his eyes forever.

She was nevertheless left a slave—a slave for life—a slave in the hands of strangers. In their hands, she saw her children, her grandchildren, and her great-grandchildren divided like so many sheep.

Worse, my grandmother, who was now very old, was thought by her new owners to be of little value. They took her to the woods, built her a little hut, and put up a little mud chimney. They made her support herself there in complete loneliness.

They virtually turned her out to die! They left her to suffer in utter loneliness, to remember and mourn over the loss of children, the loss of grandchildren, and the loss of great-grandchildren. To her—in the language of the slave's poet, Whittier—they were all gone forever:

"Gone, gone, sold and gone
To the rice swamp dank and lone,
Where the slave-whip ceaseless swings,
Where the noisome insect stings,
Where the fever-demon strews
Poison with the falling dews,
Where the sickly sunbeams glare
Through the hot and misty air—
Gone, gone, sold and gone
To the rice swamp dank and lone,
From Virginia hills and waters—
Woe is me, my stolen daughters!"

The house is empty. The children, who once sang and danced in her presence, are gone. She gropes her way, in the darkness of age, for a drink of water. Instead of the voices of her children, she hears by day the moans of the dove. By night she hears the screams of the owl. All is gloom. The grave is at the door.

Weighed down by the pains and aches of old age, she is all alone. My poor old grandmother, the devoted mother of 12 children, is left all alone, forgotten in yonder little hut.

She stands, she staggers—she falls. She groans, she dies. None of her children or grandchildren are present to wipe from her wrinkled brow the cold sweat of death.

About two years after the death of Lucretia, Master Thomas married his second wife, Rowena. She was the eldest daughter of Mr. William Hamilton. Master Thomas now lived in St. Michael's. Not long after his marriage, a misunderstanding took place between him and his brother. To punish Master Hugh, he took me from Master Hugh to live with him at St. Michael's.

Here I underwent another most painful separation. It was not so severe as the one I dreaded at the division of the property. Master Hugh and his once kind and affectionate wife had changed. The influence of brandy upon him and of slavery upon her had brought about a terrible change in both of them. So, as far as they were concerned, I thought I had little to lose by leaving.

But it was not to them that I was attached. It was to those little Baltimore boys that I felt the strongest attachment. I had received many good lessons from them and was still receiving them. The thought of leaving those boys was painful indeed.

I was leaving, too, without the hope of ever being allowed to return. Master Thomas had said he would never let me return there again. The wall between himself and his brother was still strong.

I then regretted that I had not tried to escape. The chances of escaping are ten times better from the city than from the country.

I sailed from Baltimore for St. Michael's. On the way I paid close attention to the direction the steamboats took to go to Philadelphia. I considered this knowledge would be important when the right time came to escape. When it did come, I was determined to be off.

Chapter 9 The Mean Master

I have now reached a period of my life when I can give dates. I left Baltimore and went to live with Master Thomas Auld at St. Michael's in March 1832. It was now more than seven years since I had lived with him in the family of my old master, Captain Anthony, on Colonel Lloyd's plantation.

We, of course, were now almost entire strangers to each other. He was to me a new master, as I was to him a new slave. I was ignorant of his temper and disposition, and he was equally so of mine.

We soon got know each other. I also became acquainted with his wife. They were well matched, being equally mean and cruel. I was now, for the first time in more than seven years, made to feel the painful gnawing of hunger—something I had not experienced in Baltimore.

Master Thomas was a mean man. Not to give a slave enough to eat is thought the worst form of meanness, even among slaveholders. The rule is: No matter how bad the food, let there be enough of it.

Master Thomas gave us enough of neither bad nor good food. There were four of us slaves in the kitchen—my sister Eliza, my aunt Priscilla, Priscilla's daughter Henny, and myself. We were allowed less than half a bushel of cornmeal per week and very little else. It was not enough for us to live on. We had to live at the expense of our neighbors. This we did by begging and stealing, whichever came in handy at the time of need.

A great many times we poor creatures were nearly dead with hunger, when food in abundance lay in the smokehouse. Our mistress was aware of it, but it didn't bother her.

Bad as all slaveholders are, we seldom meet one lacking every good character trait. My master was one of this rare sort. I do not know of one single noble act ever performed by him. The leading trait in his character was meanness. If there were any other element in his nature, it was made subject to this. He was mean. Like most other mean men, he lacked the ability to hide his meanness.

Captain Auld was not born a slaveholder. He had been a poor man. He came into possession of all his slaves by marriage. Of all men, adopted slaveholders are the worst.

We seldom called him "master." We generally called him "Captain Auld." He wished to have us call him "master" but lacked the firmness necessary to command us to do so. His wife used to insist upon our calling him so, but no one did.

Captain Auld was cruel, but cowardly. He commanded without firmness. At times he spoke to his slaves with the firmness of Napoleon.[1] Other times he might be mistaken for a person who had lost his way.

The luxury of having slaves of his own to wait upon him was something new, and he was unprepared for it. He was a slaveholder without the ability to hold slaves. He found himself incapable of managing his slaves either by force or fear.

In August 1832, he attended a church meeting, and there experienced religion. I had a faint hope that his

---

1. **Napoleon** Napoleon Bonaparte, Emperor of France 1804–1815

conversion would lead him to free his slaves. Even if he didn't do that, I hoped he would become more kind and humane.

I was disappointed on both counts. Religion neither made him free his slaves nor be humane to them. If it had any effect, it made him more cruel and hateful in all his ways. I believe him to have been a much worse man after his conversion than before.

Prior to his conversion, he made no excuses for his savagery. But after his conversion, he used religion to support his slaveholding cruelty.

He made the greatest play of being pious. His house was the house of prayer. He prayed morning, noon, and night. He very soon distinguished himself at church and was made a church leader.

His house was like a home for preachers. They used to take great pleasure in coming there to eat. While he starved us, he stuffed them. We have had three or four preachers there at a time.

Of those preachers, only Mr. George Cookman stands out. We slaves loved him and believed him to be a good man. We thought him instrumental in getting Mr. Samuel Harrison, a rich slaveholder, to free his slaves. We got the impression that Mr. Cookman was trying to get freedom for all slaves.

When he was at our house, we were sure to come in for prayers. When the others were there, we sometimes came in and sometimes not.

While I lived with my master in St. Michael's, I came to know a young white man, a Mr. Wilson. He proposed to keep a Sabbath school for the instruction of such slaves as might wish to learn to read the New Testament.

We met only three times. At the third meeting, Mr. West and Mr. Fairbanks, both church leaders, with many others came upon us. With sticks and stones, they drove us off and forbade us to meet again. Thus ended our little Sabbath school in the pious town of St. Michael's.

I have said that my master found religious support for his cruelty. I will give an example. I have seen him tie up a lame young woman and whip her with a cowskin, causing the warm red blood to drip. In support of the bloody deed, he would quote this passage of the Bible: "He that knoweth his master's will, and doeth it not, shall be beaten with many stripes."

Master would keep this young woman tied up in this horrid situation four or five hours at a time. I have known him to tie her up and whip her before breakfast, leave her hanging, then whip her again after dinner. He would cut her in the places already made raw with his cruel lash.

Master was cruel toward Henny because she was almost helpless. When just a child, she had fallen into the fire and burned herself horribly. Her hands were so burnt that she never got the use of them. She could do very little work, except bear heavy burdens.

Master thought she was a waste of money. Because he was a mean man, she was a constant offense to him. He gave her away once to his sister. Being a poor gift, she was sent back.

Finally, my master—to use his own words—"set her adrift to take care of herself."

My master and I had quite a number of differences. He found me unsuitable to his purposes. My city life, he said, had had an evil effect upon me. It had almost ruined me for every good purpose and fitted me for everything which was bad.

One of my greatest faults was that of letting his horse run away. It went down to his father-in-law's farm, which was about five miles from St. Michael's. I would then have to go after it.

My reason for this kind of carelessness—or carefulness—was that I could always get something to eat when I went there. Master William Hamilton, my master's father-in-law, always gave his slaves enough to eat. I never left his place hungry, no matter how quickly I needed to return.

Master Thomas finally said he would stand it no longer. I had lived with him nine months. During that time he had given me a number of severe whippings, all to no good purpose. He decided to put me out "to be broken."

For this purpose, he sent me to stay a year with Edward Covey. Mr. Covey was a poor man. He rented the farm where he lived as well as the slaves who worked on it. He had a very high reputation for breaking young slaves, which was of great value to him. Some slaveholders let Mr. Covey have their slaves for one year so he could "tame" them.

I knew about Mr. Covey and his reputation as a " nigger breaker." I knew I would at least get enough to eat, which is no small consideration to a hungry man.

Chapter 10 The Slave Breaker

I left Master Thomas's house and went to live with Mr. Covey on January 1, 1833. I was now, for the first time in my life, employed as a field hand. In my new employment, I found myself even more awkward than a country boy appeared to be in a large city.

I had been at my new home but one week before Mr. Covey gave me a very severe whipping. The lash cut my back, causing the blood to run, and raised ridges on my flesh as large as my little finger.

The details of this affair are as follows. Very early on a cold January morning, Mr. Covey sent me to the woods to get a load of wood. He gave me a team of unbroken oxen. I had never driven oxen before, and of course I was very awkward.

I succeeded in getting to the edge of the woods with little difficulty. But I had gone only a short way into the woods when the oxen became scared. They ran, pulling the cart against trees and over stumps, in the most frightful manner.

After running for a considerable distance, they finally upset the cart, dashing it with great force against a tree. Then they threw themselves into a dense thicket. How I escaped death, I do not know.

My cart was upset and shattered. My oxen were tangled among the young trees. There was no one to help me. After a long effort, I succeeded in getting my cart upright and my oxen untangled and again yoked to the cart.

I now proceeded with my team to the place where I

had been chopping wood the day before. I loaded my cart pretty heavily and then headed for home.

When I got there, I stopped my oxen to open the gate. As I did so, the oxen rushed through the gate, catching it between the wheel and the body of the cart. They tore the gate to pieces and came within a few inches of crushing me against the gatepost.

Thus twice, in one short day, I escaped death by the slightest chance.

When I told Mr. Covey what had happened and how it happened, he ordered me to return to the woods. I did so, and he followed after me. Just as I got into the woods, he came up and told me to stop my cart. He said he would teach me how to waste my time and break gates.

He then went to a tree and with his axe cut three large switches. After trimming them up neatly with his pocketknife, he ordered me to take off my clothes. I made him no answer, but stood with my clothes on.

He repeated his order. I still made him no answer, nor did I move to strip myself. Upon this, he rushed at me with the fierceness of a tiger, tore off my clothes, and lashed me till he had worn out his switches. He cut me so savagely as to leave the marks visible for a long time after. This whipping was the first of a number just like it and for similar offenses.

I lived with Mr. Covey for one year. During the first six months of that year, not a week passed without his whipping me. I was seldom free from a sore back. My awkwardness was almost always his excuse for whipping me.

Mr. Covey worked his slaves hard. He gave us enough to eat, but little time to eat it. We were often given less than five minutes to eat our meals. We were often in the field from sunrise to sunset. At haying time we often worked until midnight.

Covey would spend most of his afternoons in bed. He would then come out fresh in the evening, ready to urge us on with his words, and frequently with the whip. He was one of the few slaveholders who could and did work with his hands.

We worked in his absence almost as well as in his presence. He made us feel that he was always present with us. This he did by surprising us. He seldom openly approached the spot where we were at work.

He was so sneaky that we used to call him, among ourselves, "the snake." When we were at work in the cornfield, he would sometimes crawl on his hands and knees until he was upon us. All at once he would scream out, "Ha, ha! Come, come! Dash on, dash on!"

It was never safe to stop working for a single minute. His comings were like a thief in the night. He appeared to us as being always at hand. He was under every tree, behind every stump, in every bush, and at every window.

He would sometimes mount his horse, as if bound to St. Michael's, a distance of seven miles. Half an hour afterwards, you would see him coiled up by the corner of the fence, watching every move that we made.

Mr. Covey would say a short prayer in the morning, and a long prayer at night. Strange as it may seem, few men would at times appear more pious than he. Poor man! Such was his success at deceiving. I do believe that he sometimes deceived himself into the belief that he was a sincere worshiper of the most high God.

If I was made to suffer under slavery at any one time of my life more than another, that time was during the first six months of my stay with Mr. Covey.

We had to work in all kinds of weather. It was never

too hot or too cold to work. It could never rain, blow, hail, or snow too hard for us to work in the field. Work, work, work. The longest days were too short for Mr. Covey, and the shortest nights too long for him.

I was somewhat unmanageable when I first went there. A few months of his discipline tamed me. Mr. Covey succeeded in breaking me. I was broken in body and soul. My natural spirit was crushed. My lively mind was tamed. I no longer even cared to read. The cheerful spark in my eye died as the dark night of slavery closed in upon me. I was a man changed into a brute!

Sunday was my only free day. I spent this in a sort of beast-like stupor, half asleep under some large tree. At times I would rise up, and a flash of freedom would dart through my soul, along with a faint beam of hope. It would flicker for a moment and then vanish. I would sink down again to mourn over my hateful condition.

I was sometimes tempted to take my life—and Covey's too—but was stopped by a combination of hope and fear. My sufferings on this plantation seem now like a dream rather than a reality.

Our house stood right next to Chesapeake Bay, which was always white with sails from every part of the world. Those beautiful vessels, draped in purest white, were so delightful to the eye of free men. To me they were so many ghosts. They seemed to terrify and torment me with thoughts of my condition.

I have often been all alone on the banks of that bay and, with saddened heart and tearful eye, watched the boats sail off to the ocean.

I would cry out to them:

"You are loosened from your anchor and are free. I am tied in my chains and am a slave! You move merrily before the gentle gale, and I sadly before the

bloody whip! You are freedom's swift-winged angels that fly round the world. I am confined in bands of iron! O, that I were free! O, that I were on one of your gallant[1] decks and under your protecting wing!

"O God, save me! God, deliver me! Let me be free! Why am I a slave? I will run away. I will not stand it. I will take to the water. This very bay shall bear me into freedom. There is a better day coming."

---

1. **gallant** stately or noble in appearance

Chapter 11 The Turning Point

My condition was much worse during the first six months of my stay at Mr. Covey's than during the last six. What brought about that change is a turning point in my history.

You have seen how a man was made a slave. Now you shall see how a slave was made a man.

On one of the hottest days of August 1833, Bill Smith, William Hughes, a slave named Eli, and myself were working near the barn. About three o'clock that day, I broke down. My strength failed me, and I grew dizzy. I fell to the ground and felt as if held down by an immense weight.

I crawled to the fence that enclosed the yard, hoping to find relief from the sun. Mr. Covey came out and asked what was wrong. I told him as well as I could, for I barely had strength to speak.

He then gave me a savage kick in the side and told me to get up. I tried to do so, but fell back in the attempt. While I was lying there, Mr. Covey picked up a stick and gave me a heavy blow upon the head, making a large wound and drawing blood. He then left me there and went back to the house.

As soon as my head began to feel better, I decided to go to my master and ask for protection. A seven-mile walk was a long way in my condition.

I succeeded in getting a considerable distance on my way to the woods when Covey discovered me. He called after me to come back, threatening what he would do if I did not come. I disregarded both his calls and his threats.

Thinking I might be caught if I kept to the road, I walked through the woods. After about five hours, I arrived at Master Thomas's house. From the crown of my head to my feet, I was covered in blood. I suppose I looked like a man who had barely escaped a den of wild beasts.

I told Master Thomas everything that happened and asked him to let me get a new home. I said that if I went back to live with Mr. Covey again, he would surely kill me.

Master Thomas dismissed the idea that there was any danger of Mr. Covey's killing me. He said that he knew Mr. Covey was a good man. He would not think of taking me from him.

I stayed at St. Michael's that night. Following Master's orders, I started off to Covey's in the morning. I reached there about nine o'clock. As I drew near his house, he ran out with his cowskin to give me another whipping.

Before he could reach me, I succeeded in hiding in the cornfield. He seemed very angry and searched for me a long time. He finally gave up the chase. I suppose he thought that I would come home sooner or later for something to eat.

I spent that day mostly in the woods. I had two choices before me. I could go home and be whipped to death. Or I could stay in the woods and starve to death.

That night I ran into Sandy Jenkins. He was a slave who lived about four miles from Mr. Covey's. He said I could stay the night at his house. After we talked awhile, he said he thought I should go back to

Covey. He said that I must take a lucky root with me that would protect me from getting a whipping.

I at first thought that the simple carrying of a root in my pocket wouldn't have any such effect. But to please him, I took it.

The next day, Sunday, I started for home. On the way, I met Mr. Covey, who was going to church. He spoke to me very kindly and continued on. I began to think that there really was something in the root that Sandy had given me.

All went well till Monday morning. Long before daylight, I was called to go and rub, curry, and feed the horses. While I was doing that, Mr. Covey entered the stable with a long rope. He caught hold of my legs and tried to tie me up.

As soon as I found what he was up to, I gave a sudden jump. As I did so, I went sprawling on the stable floor. Mr. Covey seemed now to think he had me and could do what he pleased.

But at this moment—where the spirit came from, I don't know—I decided to fight. I seized Covey hard by the throat. He held on to me, and I to him. My resistance[1] was so entirely unexpected that Covey seemed surprised. He trembled like a leaf. He asked if I meant to keep up my resistance.

I told him I did, come what might. I said that he had used me like a brute for six months. I told him I was determined to be used so no longer.

We were at it for nearly two hours. Covey finally let me go, puffing and blowing at a great rate. He said that if I had not resisted, he would not have whipped me half so much.

The truth was that he had not whipped me at all. I

---

1. **resistance** act of taking a stand against; holding back

thought that he had gotten entirely the worst end of the bargain. He had drawn no blood from me, but I had from him.

The whole six months afterwards that I spent with Mr. Covey, he never laid the weight of his finger upon me in anger. He would say that sometimes he didn't want to get hold of me again.

"No," thought I, "you need not, for you will come off worse than you did before."

This battle with Mr. Covey was the turning point in my life as a slave. It lit up the few dying embers of freedom. I was feeling within me a sense of my own manhood. It brought back my self-confidence and inspired me again with an urgent need to be free.

I now resolved that, however long I might remain a slave in form, the day had passed forever when I could be a slave in fact. I did not hesitate to let it be known that the white man who expected to succeed in whipping me must also succeed in killing me.

For a long time, I was surprised that Mr. Covey did not immediately have me taken to the whipping post. After all, I had committed the crime of raising my hand against a white man in defense of myself.

I think that I was not punished because of his reputation for being a first-rate overseer and slave breaker. If people knew that he could not control a 16-year-old boy, his reputation might be ruined.

My term of actual service to Mr. Edward Covey ended on Christmas Day, 1833. The days between Christmas and New Year's Day are allowed as holidays for slaves. Those of us who had families far away were often allowed to spend the whole six days with them.

This time, however, could be spent in various ways. Some of us would keep busy making corn brooms, mats, horse collars, and baskets. Others would spend the time in hunting opossums, hares, and coons. Most slaves engaged in such sports and merriment as playing ball, wrestling, running foot races, fiddling, dancing, and drinking whisky. This last way of spending time was favored by our masters. A slave who would work during the holidays was considered by our masters as not deserving them.

The slaveholders use the holidays to keep down the spirit of freedom. If the slaveholders didn't grant holidays, you can be sure it would lead to an immediate revolt among the slaves.

Slaveholders want their slaves to spend those days in such a way as to make them as glad of their ending as of their beginning. They want to disgust their slaves with freedom by plunging them into the lowest depths. For instance, the slaveholders would give prizes to the slaves who could drink the most whisky without getting drunk. In this way they got many of us to drink to excess.

So when the holidays ended, we staggered, took a long breath, and marched to the fields. We felt rather glad to go, from what our master had deceived us into believing was freedom, back to the arms of slavery.

Chapter 12 *Thoughts of Escape*

On the first of January 1834, I left Mr. Covey's. I went to live with Mr. William Freeland, who lived about three miles from St. Michael's.

I soon found Mr. Freeland a very different man from Mr. Covey. Though not rich, he was what would be called an educated Southern gentleman. Mr. Covey, as I have shown, was a well-trained slave breaker and slave driver.

Although Mr. Freeland was a slaveholder, he seemed to have some regard for honor and justice. He had many of the faults common to slaveholders. But unlike Mr. Covey, he was open and frank. We always knew where he stood.

Very near Mr. Freeland lived the Rev. Daniel Weeden. In the same neighborhood lived the Rev. Rigby Hopkins. Mr. Weeden owned, among others, a woman slave whose name I have forgotten. This woman's back, for weeks, was kept literally raw, made so by the lash of this merciless man.

His idea was: Whether a slave behaves well or not, it is the duty of a master occasionally to whip him. Whipping reminds him of his master's authority. Such was his theory, and such was his practice.

Mr. Hopkins was even worse than Mr. Weeden. His chief boast was his ability to manage slaves. He believed in whipping slaves in advance of their deserving it. He always managed to have one or more of his slaves whipped every Monday morning.

He did this to keep them frightened. He wanted to strike terror into those who might think of escape. His plan was to whip for the small offenses in order to prevent large ones from happening. Mr. Hopkins could always find some excuse for whipping a slave.

To return to Mr. Freeland—he, like Mr. Covey, gave us enough to eat. Unlike Mr. Covey, he also gave us enough time to eat our meals.

He worked us hard but always between sunrise and sunset. He required a good deal of work to be done, but gave us good tools with which to work. His farm was large, but he employed enough people to work it with ease, compared with many of his neighbors.

My treatment, while in his employment, was heavenly compared with what I experienced at the hands of Mr. Covey.

Mr. Freeland was the owner of only two slaves. Their names were Henry Harris and John Harris. The rest of his workers he hired from other slaveholders. These consisted of myself, Sandy Jenkins, and Handy Caldwell.

Henry and John were quite intelligent. Soon after I arrived, I succeeded in creating in them a strong desire to learn how to read. This desire soon sprang up in the others also. They very soon mustered up[1] some old spelling books. I began to teach them on Sundays how to read. Some of the slaves of the neighboring farms found out what was going on and joined us.

It was understood that there must be as little display about it as possible. We did not want our masters at St. Michael's to find out. Instead of spending the Sabbath in wrestling, boxing, and drinking whisky, we were trying to learn how to read the will of God.

---

1. mustered up gathered together

I held my school at the house of a free colored man. I had at one time more than 40 students. They were of all ages, though mostly men and women.

When I think that these precious souls are today shut up in the prison house of slavery, my feelings overcome me.

These dear souls came not to school because it was popular to do so. Every moment they spent in that school, they were liable to be given 39 lashes. They came because they wished to learn. Their minds had been starved by their cruel masters. They had been shut up in mental darkness.

I kept up my school for most of the time I lived with Mr. Freeland. Besides my Sabbath school, I spent three evenings a week during the winter teaching slaves at home. I am happy to say that several of those students learned how to read. One, at least, is now free because of me.

The year passed smoothly. It seemed only about half as long as the previous year. I went through it without receiving a single blow. I will give Mr. Freeland the credit of being the best master I ever had, *until I became my own master.*

I owe the ease with which I passed the year somewhat to my fellow slaves. They were noble souls. They not only possessed loving hearts but also brave ones.

At the close of the year 1834, Mr. Freeland again hired me from my master for the year 1835. But, by this time, I began to want to live upon free land as well as with Freeland. I was no longer content, therefore, to live with him or any other slaveholder.

I began to prepare myself for a final struggle that should decide my fate one way or the other. I was approaching manhood—and I was still a slave. These thoughts moved me—I must do something. I therefore resolved that 1835 should not pass without my trying to secure my liberty.

I was not willing to seek it only for myself. My fellow slaves were dear to me. I wanted them to take part in an escape with me. I decided to find out how they felt about the idea. I began fill their minds with thoughts of freedom.

I went first to Henry, next to John, then to the others. I found in them all warm hearts and noble spirits. They were ready to hear and ready to act when a workable plan was made.

We met often and talked of our hopes and fears. We discussed the difficulties, real and imagined. At times we were almost ready to give up and to try to be content with our sorry condition. At others we were firm and unbending in our determination to go.

Our knowledge of the North did not extend farther than New York. If we went there, we could still be caught and returned to slavery. Then we would be treated ten times worse than before. The thought was truly a horrible one. It was not an idea that was easy to overcome.

When we thought of the road ahead, we were often frightened. Upon either side, we saw grim death taking the most horrid shapes. Now it was starvation causing us to eat our own flesh. Now it was giant waves and we were drowning. Now we were overtaken and torn to pieces by the fangs of the terrible bloodhound.

We were stung by scorpions. We swam in rivers, encountered wild beasts, slept in the woods, suffered hunger and nakedness. Then we were caught by those who were chasing us. In our resistance, we were shot dead upon the spot!

These pictures sometimes terrified us, and made us:

"rather bear those ills we had,
Than fly to others, that we knew not of."

Chapter 13 The Escape Plan

In deciding to run away, we did more than Patrick Henry.[1] It was a doubtful liberty at most. It was almost certain death if we failed. For my part, I should prefer death to hopeless bondage.

Our group consisted of Henry Harris, John Harris, Henry Bailey, Charles Roberts, and myself. Our plan was to take a large canoe belonging to Mr. Hamilton. On the Saturday night before the Easter holidays, we would paddle up the Chesapeake Bay. When we got to the head of the bay—a distance of 70 or 80 miles—we would turn our canoe adrift. Then we would follow the North Star till we got beyond the limits of Maryland.

Our reason for taking the water route was that we were less likely to be suspected as runaways. We hoped to be regarded as fishermen. If we took the land route, we would be stopped for any number of reasons. Any white person could stop us and question us.

The week before our intended start, I wrote several passes, one for each of us. As well as I can remember, they were in the following words:

"This is to certify that I, the undersigned, have given the bearer, my servant, full liberty to go to Baltimore and spend the Easter holidays. Written with mine own hand, 1835.

William Hamilton
Near St. Michael's, in Talbot County, Maryland."

---

1. **Patrick Henry** 18th-century American patriot who said, "Give me liberty or give me death."

We were not going *to* Baltimore, but up the Bay *toward* Baltimore. These passes were only intended to protect us while on the Bay.

As the time drew near for us to escape, our anxiety became more and more intense. But every man stood firm.

We were to leave Saturday night. Friday night was a sleepless one for me. I probably felt more anxious than the rest because I was at the head of the whole plan.

After a painful waiting, Saturday came. Early in the morning, we went as usual to the field. As we worked, I had a strange feeling.

I turned to Sandy—who was not part of the plan, but knew of it—and said, "We are betrayed!"

"Well," said he, "that thought has this moment struck me."

We said no more, but I was never more certain of anything.

The horn was blown as usual, and we went up from the field to the house for breakfast. Just as I got near the house, I saw four white men with two colored men. The white men were on horseback, and the colored ones were walking behind, as if tied.

I watched them a few moments till they got up to our gate. There they halted and tied the colored men to the gatepost.

In a few moments, up to the house rode Mr. Hamilton, one of the four white men, and asked for Mr. Freeland.

After he, Mr. Freeland, and the three other men talked for a while, they all walked up to the kitchen door.

There was no one in the kitchen but myself and John. Henry and Sandy were up at the barn. Mr. Freeland put his head in at the door and called me by name. He said there were some gentlemen at the door who wished to see me.

I stepped to the door and asked what they wanted. They at once seized me and tied me. They lashed my hands closely together.

I asked what was the matter. They said they had learned I had been in a "scrape" and wanted to ask me some questions.

In a few moments, they succeeded in tying John. They then turned to Henry, who had by this time returned. They told him to cross his hands.

"I won't!" said Henry, in a firm tone.

"Won't you?" said Tom Graham, the constable.

"No, I won't!" said Henry in a still stronger tone.

With this, two of the constables pulled out their shining pistols. They swore that they would make him cross his hands or kill him. Each one cocked his pistol. With fingers on the trigger, they walked up to Henry, saying together that if he did not cross his hands, they would blow his heart out.

"Shoot me, shoot me!" said Henry. "You can't kill me but once. Shoot, shoot—but I *won't be tied!*"

With a single stroke as quick as lightning, he dashed the pistols from the hand of each constable. As he did this all the white men fell upon him. After beating him some time, they finally overpowered him and got him tied.

During the fight, I managed to get my pass out, and, without being discovered, put it into the fire.

We were all now tied, and just as we were to leave for Easton Jail, Betsy Freeland, mother of William Freeland, came to the door with her hands full of biscuits. She divided them between Henry and John.

She then said to me: "You devil! You yellow devil! It was you that put it into the heads of Henry and John to run away. It's because of you, you long-legged devil. Henry and John would never have thought of such a thing."

I made no reply, and we were immediately hurried off towards St. Michael's.

About halfway to St. Michael's, while the constables in charge were looking ahead, Henry asked me what he should do with his pass. I told him to eat it with his biscuit, and admit nothing.

We passed the word around, *"Admit nothing."* *"Admit nothing!"* we all said. Our confidence in each other was unshaken. We were going to succeed or fail together.

When we reached St. Michael's, we were given a sort of trial. We all denied that we ever intended to run away. We did this more to find out what evidence they had against us than from any hope of being cleared.

We found the evidence against us to be the word of one person. Our master would not tell who it was.

We were sent off to Easton. When we got there, we were delivered to the sheriff, Mr. Joseph Graham, and placed in jail. Henry, John, and myself were placed in one room together. Charles and Henry Bailey were placed in another.

We had not been in jail 20 minutes when a swarm of slave-traders and agents for slave-traders flocked into jail to look at us and to see if we were for sale. They laughed and grinned over us, saying, "Ah, my boys! We have got you, haven't we?" After taunting us in various ways, they one by one questioned us, with intent to find out our value.

They rudely asked us if we would not like to have them for our masters. We didn't answer them.

On Monday, Mr. Hamilton and Mr. Freeland came up to Easton and took Charles, the two Henrys, and John out of jail. They took them home, leaving me alone.

I regarded this separation as a final one. It caused me more pain than anything else that happened. I supposed they had decided that I was the one behind the whole plan to run away. I guessed that they would sell me to a slave-trader as a warning to the others.

I was kept in jail about one week. Finally Captain Auld, my master, to my surprise, came and took me out.

I thought he might sell me to a slave-trader. At best, I thought, he would keep me at St. Michael's. Instead, he decided to send me back to Baltimore to live again with his brother Hugh and to learn a trade. There was so great a prejudice against me in the community of St. Michael's that he feared I might be killed.

Three years and one month had passed. I was once more permitted to return to my old home at Baltimore.

Chapter 14 Learning a Trade

A few weeks after, I went to Baltimore. Master Hugh hired me out to Mr. William Gardner, a shipbuilder. I was put there to learn how to caulk.[1]

It did not work out well. Mr. Gardner was hired to build two large ships for the Mexican government. They were supposed to be finished by July. If they were not ready by then, Mr. Gardner would lose a large sum of money.

So when I started there, all was hurry. There was no time to learn anything. Every man had to do what he already knew how to do.

Mr. Gardner told me to do whatever the carpenters ordered me to do. This was placing me at the call of about 75 men. I was to regard all these as masters. Their word was to be my law.

My situation was a most trying one. At times, I needed a dozen pairs of hands. I was called a dozen ways in the space of a single minute. Three or four voices would strike my ear at the same moment.

It was "Fred, come carry this timber yonder."— "Fred, bring that roller here."—"Fred, go get a fresh can of water."—"I say, darky, blast your eyes, why don't you heat up some pitch?"—"Hello! hello! hello!" (Three voices at the same time.) "Come here!—Go there!— Hold on where you are! If you move, I'll knock your brains out!"

---

1. **caulk** to fill or seal cracks, such as those in a wooden ship's hull

This was my school for eight months. I might have remained there longer except for a terrible fight I had with four of the white apprentices. My left eye was nearly knocked out. I was horribly beaten.

The facts were these. Until a very little while after I arrived there, white and black ship's carpenters worked side by side, and no one seemed to mind. Many of the black carpenters were free men.

Things were going along very well. All at once, the white carpenters said they would not work with free colored workmen. Their reason was that they feared free colored carpenters would soon take over all the work. Then poor white men would be out of work. They therefore felt called upon at once to put a stop to it.

They told Mr. Gardner they would work no longer unless he fired his black carpenters.

Although this did not apply directly to me, my fellow apprentices began to feel it was degrading to work with me. They began talk about the "niggers" taking over the country. They said we all ought to be killed.

They made my condition as hard as they could by ordering me around rudely and sometimes striking me. I, of course, kept the vow I made after the fight with Mr. Covey and struck back.

As long as I kept them from getting together against me, I succeeded very well. I could whip any of them, taking them separately. They, however, finally combined and came upon me, armed with sticks, stones, and heavy handspikes. One came in toward me with a half brick. There was one at each side of me and one behind me. While I was fighting those in front and on either side, the one behind ran up with the handspike. He struck me a heavy blow upon the head.

It stunned me. I fell, and then they all attacked me, beating me with their fists. I let them continue for a while, as I gathered strength. Then I gave a sudden push and rose to my hands and knees. Just as I did that, one of them gave me a powerful kick in the left eye.

My eyeball seemed to burst. When they saw my eye closed and badly swollen, they left me. I then seized the handspike and pursued them for a time. But then the carpenters interfered, so I thought I might as well give it up. It was impossible to stand up against so many.

All this took place in front of not less than 50 white ship's carpenters. Not one said a friendly word. Some cried, "Kill the nigger! Kill him! Kill him! He struck a white person!"

I found my only chance for life was in flight. I succeeded in getting away without an additional blow.

I went directly home and told the story of my wrongs to Master Hugh. He listened carefully and expressed a lot of anger at what happened.

The heart of my once-kind mistress was again melted into pity. My puffed eye and blood-covered face moved her to tears. She sat near me and washed the blood from my face. With a mother's tenderness, she bandaged my head.

Master Hugh was very angry. He poured out curses upon the heads of those who did the deed.

As soon as I felt a little better, he took me with him to a lawyer. He wanted to see what could be done about the matter.

The lawyer said he could do nothing unless some white man would come forward and testify. Even if I had been killed in the presence of 1,000 colored people, their testimony would not count.

Master Hugh, for once, was forced to say this state of things was too bad.

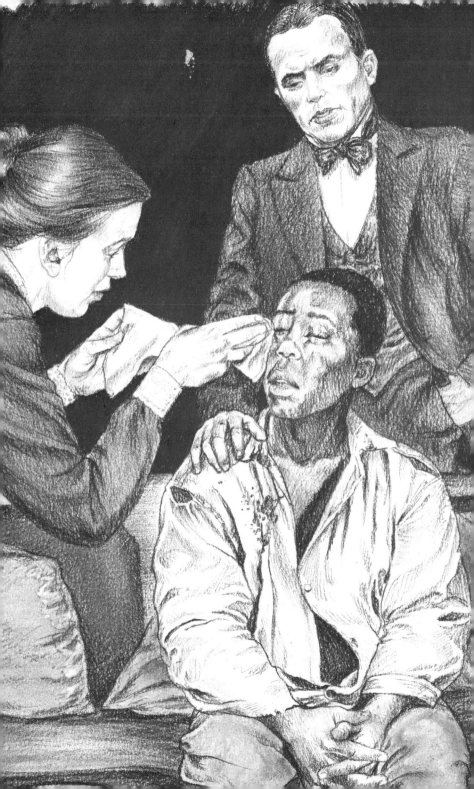

Of course, it was impossible to get any white man to testify on my behalf and against the young white men. Even those who may have felt sorry for me were not prepared to do this.

At that time, the slightest show of humanity toward a colored person was called *abolitionism*. No one wanted to be connected to that.

Nothing was done, and probably nothing would have been done even if I had been killed. Such was and such remains the state of things.

Master Hugh refused to let me go back again to Mr. Gardner. I stayed at home, and his wife dressed my wound till I was again restored to health.

Master Hugh then took me into the shipyard of which he was foreman. There I was immediately set to caulking. Very soon I learned the art of using my mallet and irons.

In the course of one year from the time I left Mr. Gardner's, I was able to command the highest wages given to the most experienced caulkers.

I was now of some importance to my master. He would hire me out, and I could usually bring him from $6 to $7 per week. My wages were $1.50 a day, and I sometimes brought him $9 per week

After learning how to caulk, I looked for jobs on my own. I made my own contracts and collected the money which I earned. My pathway became much more smooth than before. My condition was now much more comfortable. When I could get no caulking to do, I did nothing.

While working for Mr. Gardner, I had been kept so busy I could think of nothing. Now, during my leisure time, those old notions about freedom would come over me again.

I have observed this in my experience of slavery: Whenever my condition was improved, it only increased my desire to be free instead of increasing my contentment. It set me to thinking of plans to gain my freedom.

I have found that, to make a contented slave, it is necessary to make an unthinking one. It is necessary to darken his moral and mental vision. As far as possible, it is necessary to wipe out the power of reason. He must be made to feel that slavery is right. He can be brought to that only when he ceases to be a man.

I was now getting, as I have said, $1.50 per day. I contracted for it. I earned it. It was paid to me. It was rightfully my own. Yet, upon returning home each Saturday night, I had to deliver every cent of that money to Master Hugh.

Why?

Not because he earned it—not because he had any hand in earning it—not because I owed it to him—not because he possessed the slightest shadow of a right to it.

It was solely because he had the power to force me to give it up. The right of the grim pirate upon the high seas is exactly the same.

Chapter 15 Escape from Slavery

I now come to that part of my life during which I finally succeeded in making my escape from slavery. But before I tell any of the details, I think I should let you know of my intention not to give all the facts about the escape.

My reasons for taking this course are as follows. First, if I were to give a full statement of the facts, it is very likely that some of the people who helped me could be hurt.

Second, such a statement would surely bring about greater watchfulness on the part of slaveholders than ever before. That, of course, would give them the means of guarding a door through which some dear brother bondman[1] might escape his chains.

I deeply regret that I have to hide what happened during my escape. I know that many people would be interested in reading an accurate statement of all the facts. It would give me great pleasure indeed to satisfy their curiosity.

I must deprive myself of this pleasure. I must not risk closing the slightest avenue by which a brother slave might clear himself of the chains of slavery. I must keep the merciless slaveholder ignorant of the means of flight adopted by the slave.

But enough of this. I will now proceed to the facts that I can reveal of my escape. I am alone responsible

---

1. **bondman** a person who serves others without pay; a slave

for my escape. No one can be made to suffer for it but myself.

Early in 1838, I became quite restless. I could see no reason why I should pour the reward of my work into the purse of my master. When I carried my weekly wages to him, he would count the money. Then he would look me in the face with a robber-like fierceness and ask, "Is this all?"

He was satisfied with nothing less than the last cent. He would, however, when I made him $6, sometimes give me six cents to encourage me. It had the opposite effect. I regarded it as a sort of admission of my right to the whole.

My discontent grew. I was always on the lookout for a way to escape. Finding no direct means, I decided to look for work so I could save money with which to make my escape.

When Master Thomas came to Baltimore to purchase his spring goods, I asked him to allow me to hire my time. He refused my request, saying it was another trick by which to escape. He told me I could go nowhere on my own. He said that, if I ran away, he would spare no effort to catch me.

He told me to be satisfied and obedient. He told me that to be happy, I must lay out no plans for the future. He said that if I behaved myself properly, he would take care of me.

In spite of him and even in spite of myself, I continued to think about the injustice of my enslavement and how to escape.

About two months after this, I applied to Master Hugh for hiring time. He did not know that I had already asked Master Thomas and had been refused. After some thought, he granted me the privilege. He gave it to me on the following terms: I was to make all contracts with those for whom I worked and find my own jobs. In return, I was to pay him $3 each week and pay for my own caulking tools, my board, and my clothing.

My board was $2.50 per week. This, with the wear and tear of clothing and caulking tools, made my regular expenses about $6 per week. This amount I was ordered to pay him, or give up the privilege of hiring my time.

Rain or shine, work or no work, at the end of each week I had to pay him the money or give up my privilege. This arrangement was decidedly in my master's favor. It relieved him of all need of looking after me. His money was sure. He received all the benefits of slaveholding without having to support me. I had the worries of a free man, but I was still a slave.

I found it a hard bargain. But hard as it was, I thought it better than the old way of getting along. It was a step towards freedom to be allowed to bear the responsibilities of a free man.

I set out to make money. Working night and day, I earned enough to meet my expenses and to save a little money every week.

I went on this way from May till August. Master Hugh then refused to allow me to hire my time any longer. The grounds for his refusal was a failure on my part, one Saturday, to bring him my pay.

During that week, I had arranged with a number of friends to go to a meeting about ten miles from Baltimore. I was late getting off work Saturday evening and was unable to get down to Master Hugh's without disappointing my friends.

I knew that Master Hugh was in no special need of the money that night. I therefore decided to go to the meeting and pay him the $3 upon my return. I stayed at the meeting a day longer than I intended. But as soon as I returned, I went to pay him what was due.

I found him very angry. He said he had a great mind to give me a whipping. He wished to know how I dared leave the city without his permission.

I told him that I had always paid him what was due but did not know that I had to ask him when and where I should go.

This reply troubled him. He said that after this week I could hire my time no longer because the next thing he knew, I would be running away. Then he told me to bring my tools and clothing home.

I did so. However, I spent the whole week without doing a single stroke of work. I did this to get back at him.

On Saturday night, he asked for my week's wages. I told him I had no wages—I had done no work that week.

We nearly came to blows. He shouted and swore at me. He did not strike me but told me that he would see to it that I worked regularly from now on. I thought the matter over during the next day and chose the third day of September for my second escape attempt.

I now had three weeks to prepare for my journey. Early on Monday morning, before Master Hugh had time to find work for me, I went out and found work myself. Mr. Butler hired me to work at his shipyard near the drawbridge, upon what is called the City Block. At the end of the week, I brought Master Hugh between $8 and $9.

He seemed pleased, and asked me why I had not done the same the week before. Little did he know what my plans were. My purpose in working steadily was to remove any suspicion he might have that I might run away. In this I succeeded. He thought I was never more satisfied than at the very time during which I was planning my escape.

The second week passed, and again I brought him my full wages. So well pleased was he that he gave me 25 cents. This was quite a large sum for a slave-holder to give a slave. He told me to make good use of it. I told him I would.

Things went very smoothly indeed, but within me there was trouble. I had a number of friends in Baltimore that I loved. The thought of leaving them forever was painful.

Besides the pain of separation, I feared failure. I felt sure that, if I failed in this attempt, my case would be a hopeless one. It would seal my fate as a slave forever. I could not hope to get off with anything less than the harshest punishment.

But I remained firm, and, as I had planned, I left my chains on the third day of September, 1838. I succeeded in reaching New York without the slightest interruption of any kind. How I did so—my strategy, my route, and my transportation—I must leave unexplained for the reasons before mentioned.

Chapter 16 A New Life

I have been frequently asked how I felt when I found myself in a free state. It was a moment of the highest excitement I ever experienced.

In writing to a dear friend, immediately after my arrival in New York, I said I felt like one who had escaped a den of hungry lions. That feeling, however, very soon left me. I was again seized with a feeling of great insecurity and loneliness.

I could still be kidnapped and taken back to Maryland. Then I would have to suffer all the tortures of slavery once again. This thought in itself was enough to dampen my spirit. The loneliness was even worse. There I was among thousands, and yet was a perfect stranger without home and without friends.

I was afraid to speak to anyone for fear of falling into the hands of money-loving kidnappers, whose business was to lie in wait for fugitive slaves.[1]

"Trust no man!" This was the motto I adopted when I departed from slavery. I saw in every white man an enemy, and in almost every colored man cause for distrust.

It was a most painful situation. To understand it, you must experience it or imagine yourself in a similar situation. Picture yourself as a fugitive slave in a strange land—where at any moment

---

1. **fugitive slaves** runaway slaves

you can be seized by your fellow men. Then you will fully understand the hardships of, and sympathize with, the life of the fugitive slave.

Thank Heaven, I was in this situation only for a short time. I was saved from it by the hand of Mr. David Ruggles. His kindness I shall never forget.

I had been in New York only a few days when Mr. Ruggles sought me out. He very kindly took me to his boardinghouse. He asked me where I wanted to go. He thought it would be unsafe for me to remain in New York. I told him I was a caulker and would go where I could get work. I thought of Canada, but he suggested I go to New Bedford, Massachusetts. I would have a good chance to get work there.

At this time my intended wife, Anna, a free woman, came from Baltimore and joined me in New York. A few days after her arrival, we were married. Upon receiving the marriage certificate and $5 from Mr. Ruggles, we set out by steamboat for Newport, Rhode Island. From there, we took a stagecoach to New Bedford.

Upon reaching New Bedford, we were directed to the house of Mr. and Mrs. Nathan Johnson. We were kindly received and provided for. They proved themselves quite worthy of the name *abolitionists*.

On the morning after our arrival at New Bedford, the question arose as to what name I should use. The name given me by my mother was Frederick Augustus Washington Bailey. I, however, had dropped the two middle names years earlier and was generally known as Frederick Bailey.

I gave Mr. Johnson the privilege of choosing a name for me. I told him he must not take from me the name of Frederick. I had to hold on to that in order to preserve a sense of my identity. He had just been reading "The Lady of the Lake"[2] and suggested that I take the name of Douglass. From that time until now, I have been called Frederick Douglass.

While I was in slavery, I had thought that few of the comforts and luxuries of life were enjoyed by whites in the North. I probably got this idea from the fact that Northern people owned no slaves. I imagined Northern whites were about on a level with the exceedingly poor non-slaveholding population of the South. I believed that, in the absence of slaves, there could be no wealth and very few luxuries. I expected to meet with a rough population in the North. I was mistaken.

On the afternoon of the day when I reached New Bedford, I visited the wharves in order to view the shipping. Here I found myself surrounded with the strongest proofs of wealth. In the harbor, I saw many of the finest ships. Large warehouses filled with the necessities and comforts of life were everywhere here.

Added to this, almost everybody seemed to be at work quietly, compared with what I was used to in Baltimore. There were no loud songs coming from those engaged in loading and unloading ships. I heard no deep oaths or horrid curses aimed at the laborer. I saw no whipping of men.

Every man appeared to understand his work. He did it with a sober yet cheerful look and with a sense of his own dignity as a man. To me, this looked very

---

2. **"The Lady of the Lake"** a long narrative poem written in 1810 by Sir Walter Scott

strange. From the wharves, I strolled around the town. I gazed with wonder and admiration at the splendid churches, beautiful houses, and fine gardens.

Everything looked clean, new, and beautiful. I saw few or no broken-down houses, no half-naked children and barefoot women. All of these I had been used to seeing in Hillsborough, Easton, St. Michael's, and Baltimore.

The most surprising as well as the most interesting thing to me was the condition of the colored people. Many of them—like myself—had escaped from the South. Many, who had not been seven years out of their chains, lived in finer houses and enjoyed more of the comforts of life than the average slaveholder in Maryland.

My friend, Mr. Johnson, lived in a neater house, dined at a better table, read more newspapers, and better understood the condition of the nation than nine-tenths of the slaveholders in Talbot County. Yet he was a working man, his hands hardened by toil.

I found work the third day after my arrival, loading a sloop with barrels of oil. It was dirty, hard work for me, but I went at it with a glad heart and a willing hand. I was now my own master. It was a happy moment, the joy of which can be understood only by those who have been slaves. It was the first work, the reward of which was to be entirely my own. There was no Master Hugh standing ready, the moment I earned the money, to rob me of it.

I worked that day with a pleasure I had never before experienced. I was at work for myself and for my new wife. It was the starting point of a new life.

When I got through with that job, I could find no work as a caulker. Mr. Johnson kindly let me have his sawhorse and saw. I very soon found myself plenty of work. There was no work too hard—none too dirty. I was ready to saw wood, shovel coal, sweep chimneys, or roll oil barrels. I did all of these for nearly three years, before I became known to the anti-slavery world.

About four months after I went to New Bedford, I began to read the *Liberator*, a weekly anti-slavery newspaper. The paper became my meat and my drink. My soul was set all on fire. Its sympathy for my brothers in bonds—its attacks on slaveholders, its exposures of slavery—sent a thrill of joy through me such as I had never felt before!

I soon got a fairly correct idea of the principles, measures, and spirit of the anti-slavery movement. I took hold of the cause. I could do little. What I could, I did with a joyful heart, and never felt happier than when in an anti-slavery meeting. I seldom said much at the meetings because what I wanted to say was said so much better by others.

While attending an anti-slavery convention at Nantucket, on the 11th of August, 1841, I felt strongly moved to speak. I was urged to do so by Mr. William C. Coffin, a gentleman who had heard me speak in the colored people's meeting at New Bedford.

The truth was that I still felt like a slave, and the idea of speaking to white people weighed me down. I spoke for only a few moments. When I felt a degree of freedom, I said what I desired with considerable ease.

From that time until now, I have been engaged in pleading the cause of my brothers—with how much success and devotion I leave those acquainted with my labors to decide.

Appendix

I find in reading over the foregoing Narrative that I have, in several instances, spoken harshly about religion. That may lead those who do not know my religious views to suppose that I am against all religion.

What I have said against religion, I mean strictly to apply to the *slaveholding religion* of this land. I love the pure, peaceable, and impartial Christianity of Christ. The difference between the two is so wide that to receive the one as good, pure, and holy is of necessity to reject the other as bad, corrupt, and wicked.

I can see no reason but the most deceitful one for calling that religion Christianity. The slaveholding type of religion gives us the man who robs me of my earnings at the end of each week and meets me as a church leader on Sunday morning.

It is against such religion that I have felt it my duty to testify.

I sincerely hope that this little book may do something toward throwing light on the American slave system. I hope it will speed the glad day of deliverance to the millions of my brothers in bonds.

Faithfully relying upon the power of truth, love, and justice, for success in my humble efforts—and pledging myself anew to the sacred cause—I subscribe myself,

FREDERICK DOUGLASS
Lynn, Mass., April 28, 1845

REVIEWING YOUR READING

Chapters 1–2

FINDING THE MAIN IDEA

1. Chapter 1 mostly tells about Douglass's
(A) sister (B) early life (C) school days (D) travels.

2. A good title for Chapter 2 might be
(A) City Life (B) Runaway Slaves (C) The Civil War
(D) Plantation Life.

REMEMBERING DETAILS

3. One cause of Douglass's unhappiness as a child is that he doesn't know
(A) his grandmother (B) his way to the grocery store
(C) the date of his birthday (D) who his mother is.

4. Douglass hides in the closet when
(A) his aunt is whipped (B) it is time to work (C) school starts (D) there is a thunderstorm.

5. At the Big House Farm, slaves are given clothes
(A) twice a year (B) when they need them (C) yearly
(D) every three months.

6. Slaves consider doing errands at the Great House Farm to be
(A) dangerous (B) a privilege (C) tiring (D) shameful.

DRAWING CONCLUSIONS

7. You can guess that Douglass finds his new life on the main plantation
(A) boring (B) fun (C) terrifying (D) about the same as at his grandmother's.

8. Douglass thinks that the overseer, Mr. Severe,
(A) deserves his name (B) takes no pleasure in whipping slaves (C) hates violence (D) is fair.

USING YOUR REASON

9. Captain Anthony is angry at Hester because he was
(A) tired (B) jealous (C) scared (D) just doing his job.

10. The Great House Farm seems almost like
(A) a big city (B) a village (C) a small farm (D) a cattle ranch.

THINKING IT OVER

1. Why do you think Douglass's master didn't allow slaves to ask questions? How would you feel if you couldn't ask questions about your own life?

2. What part did singing play in the life of a slave? Explain.

Chapters 3–4

FINDING THE MAIN IDEA

1. Chapters 3 and 4 are mostly about
   (A) the treatment of slaves (B) the government in Maryland
   (C) Douglass's mother (D) gardening.

REMEMBERING DETAILS

2. To keep slaves from stealing fruit, Colonel Lloyd
   (A) locks them up (B) puts tar on a fence (C) puts guard dogs in the orchards (D) hires a watchman.

3. Old Barney and his son take care of
   (A) the garden (B) the tar supply (C) the horses
   (D) the young slaves.

4. When Demby disobeys Mr. Gore, Mr. Gore
   (A) whips him (B) sells him (C) forgives him (D) kills him.

5. Mrs. Hicks kills a slave girl because she
   (A) fell asleep (B) ran away (C) stole (D) lied.

DRAWING CONCLUSIONS

6. Douglass thinks that when slaves talk about their owners to white people, the best policy is to
   (A) tell the truth (B) say their owners are kind (C) ask for protection (D) pretend to be deaf.

7. For whites to kill slaves in Talbot County, it is
   (A) punishable by death (B) unheard of (C) not treated as a crime (D) cause for imprisonment.

USING YOUR REASON

8. When Colonel Lloyd finds something wrong with a slave, the slave
   (A) has to defend himself (B) can talk his way out of it
   (C) needs a lawyer (D) has to be silent.

9. When Mr. Gore treats slaves savagely, he
(A) gets red in the face (B) shows no emotion (C) apologizes
(D) asks Colonel Lloyd's permission first.

THINKING IT OVER

1. Colonel Lloyd tricked a slave into talking against him and then punished him. What does that tell you about the kind of person Colonel Lloyd was?

2. What excuses does Mr. Gore give for his treatment of Demby? How is this effective?

Chapters 5–6

FINDING THE MAIN IDEA

1. Chapter 5 is mostly about
(A) farming methods (B) Douglass's feelings about leaving the plantation (C) horses (D) slave clothing.

2. Chapter 6 is mostly about
(A) Colonel Lloyd (B) memories of his mother (C) sailing on Chesapeake Bay (D) his new life in a city.

REMEMBERING DETAILS

3. Daniel Lloyd used to
(A) whip Douglass (B) protect Douglass (C) mistreat Demby
(D) take care of chickens.

4. When he is told he is going to Baltimore, Douglass
(A) is scared (B) is happy (C) cries (D) hides in the closet.

5. When Douglass meets Mrs. Auld, he thinks her
(A) cold (B) funny looking (C) kindhearted (D) cruel.

6. Compared to a country slave, a city slave is
(A) better off (B) lazier (C) worse off (D) treated about the same.

DRAWING CONCLUSIONS

7. Douglass feels that he
(A) is the same as other slaves (B) is unluckier than other slaves (C) will always be a slave (D) will someday be free

8. When Douglass's reading lessons are stopped, he decides he
(A) doesn't need to read (B) can read well enough (C) will go to night school (D) will teach himself.

USING YOUR REASON

9. When Douglass sails to Baltimore, he goes from the rear of the boat to the bow because
(A) he is seasick (B) that is the slave section (C) he isn't interested in what is behind him (D) he can fish from the bow.

10. The main influence that changes Mrs. Auld for the worse is
(A) her husband (B) Douglass's behavior (C) the Baltimore weather (D) the system of slavery.

THINKING IT OVER

1. Douglass didn't feel the least bit unhappy about leaving his home and going to Baltimore. Use examples from the text that explain why.

2. Hugh Auld didn't think slaves should learn to read. Why? How did this affect Douglass's desire to learn to read?

Chapters 7–8

FINDING THE MAIN IDEA

1. Chapter 7 is mostly about
(A) Douglass's education (B) plantation life (C) hunting and fishing (D) the Great House Farm.

2. Chapter 8 is mostly about
(A) a funeral (B) how slaves are treated when their owner dies (C) sailing on Chesapeake Bay (D) Douglass's first pair of trousers.

REMEMBERING DETAILS

3. Mrs. Auld gets most angry when she sees Douglass
(A) getting up late (B) staying out late (C) reading the newspaper (D) hitting her son.

4. In trade for reading lessons, Douglass gives white boys
(A) fishing lessons (B) money (C) bread (D) fruit.

5. At the "valuation," slaves are treated like
(A) property (B) kings (C) human beings (D) guests.

6. When Douglass is sent from Baltimore to St. Michael's, he mostly misses
(A) Mrs. Auld (B) Mr. Auld (C) the Baltimore weather (D) the little Baltimore boys.

DRAWING CONCLUSIONS

7. You can guess that Douglass thinks abolitionists
   (A) were crazy (B) had good ideas (C) were troublemakers
   (D) were of no importance to him.

8. Douglass thinks being sold in Georgia would be harder for
   him than for plantation slaves because
   (A) he likes cool weather (B) he has no friends there
   (C) he is used to kind treatment (D) he is a Yankee.

USING YOUR REASON

9. From the writing on ship's timbers, Douglass learns
   (A) to build ships (B) to keep out of the way (C) to write
   letters of the alphabet (D) to sail.

10. Douglass pays attention to the direction steamboats for
    Philadelphia take because it will be useful
    (A) to the boys in Baltimore (B) when he makes his escape
    (C) in learning to sail (D) to Mr. Auld.

THINKING IT OVER

1. Why did the book *The Columbian Orator* have such a strong
   influence on Douglass? Explain.

2. Douglass thinks slavery brutalizes both the slave and the
   slaveholder. Do you agree? Back up your argument with
   examples from Chapter 7.

Chapters 9–10

FINDING THE MAIN IDEA

1. Chapter 9 is mostly about
   (A) Master Thomas Auld (B) learning to read (C) his
   grandmother (D) city life.

2. Chapter 10 is mostly about
   (A) life on Mr. Covey's farm (B) the valuation
   (C) Douglass's reading lessons (D) raising horses.

REMEMBERING DETAILS

3. Master Thomas Auld never gives slaves
   (A) a hard time (B) enough to eat (C) lectures (D) any work
   to do.

4. Master Thomas Auld sometimes justifies beating slaves by quoting
   (A) the Slave Manual (B) his mother (C) the law
   (D) the Bible.

5. Douglass has a hard time driving oxen because he
   (A) is afraid of cattle (B) had burned his hands (C) had never done it before (D) is so tired.

6. Douglass is tormented by the sight of
   (A) slave-traders in Georgia (B) pretty women in Baltimore
   (C) oxen (D) sailboats on Chesapeake Bay.

DRAWING CONCLUSIONS

7. Douglass felt Mr. Thomas Auld and his wife are well matched because they are both
   (A) Yankees (B) mean and cruel (C) white (D) afraid of Mr. Covey.

8. The slaves have a nickname for Mr. Covey because he is so
   (A) sneaky (B) reasonable (C) fat (D) lazy.

USING YOUR REASON

9. The slaves like Mr. Cookman because
   (A) they think he wants to free all slaves (B) he jokes a lot
   (C) he had once been a slave (D) he is from Georgia.

10. Douglass is awkward when he goes to work for Mr. Covey because he
    (A) is lame (B) has big feet (C) has never done field work
    (D) has a bad attitude.

THINKING IT OVER

1. When Douglass lived with Thomas Auld, he had to steal to get enough to eat. How did that affect Douglass? Do you think he was wrong?

2. For Douglass the sailing ships were symbols of freedom. What might some other symbols of freedom be? What might some symbols of slavery be?

Chapters 11–12

FINDING THE MAIN IDEA

1. Chapter 11 is mostly about how Douglass
   (A) becomes a man (B) learns to obey (C) learns to write
   (D) becomes an oxen driver.

2. Chapter 12 is mostly about how Douglass develops
(A) his farming skills (B) a heart condition (C) ideas about
being his own master (D) a love for the outdoors.

REMEMBERING DETAILS

3. When Douglass gets dizzy and falls, Mr. Covey
(A) helps him up (B) feels sorry for him (C) laughs at him
(D) kicks and hits him.

4. At the Christmas holidays, the slave owners want the slaves to
(A) drink to excess (B) get nice gifts (C) keep working
(D) go to church.

5. Mr. Freeland does not
(A) give slaves time to eat (B) give slaves good food
(C) pretend to be religious (D) act open and frank.

6. Until Douglass became his own master, his best master was
(A) Mr. Hopkins (B) Mr. Covey (C) Captain Anthony
(D) Mr. Freeland.

DRAWING CONCLUSIONS

7. When it came to fighting, you can guess Douglass
(A) is not good at it (B) is a tough fighter (C) is afraid to
fight (D) doesn't think he should fight.

8. Douglass taught other slaves to read
(A) to impress their masters (B) because it was popular
to do so (C) because he felt it was important, and they wished
to learn (D) to avoid getting whipped.

USING YOUR REASON

9. After his fight with Covey, Douglass
(A) becomes obedient (B) grows more independent
(C) vows never to fight again (D) loses his courage.

10. The slaves who come to Douglass's school
(A) take a big risk (B) do it for fun (C) do it to be popular
(D) never learn much.

THINKING IT OVER

1. What happens to Douglass when Mr. Covey tries to tie him up
and whip him?

2. Douglass says fears of the unknown often kept slaves from
trying to escape. Have you ever been kept from doing something you wanted to do because of such fears? Discuss.

Chapters 13–14

FINDING THE MAIN IDEA

1. Chapter 13 is mostly about Douglass's
   (A) hunt for work (B) failed escape attempt (C) school for slaves (D) visit to St. Michael's.

2. Chapter 14 is mostly about Douglass's experiences
   (A) as a paid worker (B) in the Easton jail (C) in planning an escape (D) with a slave breaker.

REMEMBERING DETAILS

3. Douglass gets rid of his fake pass by
   (A) hiding it in his hat (B) swallowing it (C) giving it to Betsy Freeland (D) putting it in a fire.

4. In the jail, the slaves are visited by
   (A) Georgia slave-traders (B) ministers (C) Sandy Jenkins (D) Mrs. Auld.

5. Douglass goes to Gardner's shipyard to
   (A) wash floors (B) be a servant (C) learn how to caulk (D) learn how to sail.

6. When four men beat up Douglass, Mrs. Auld
   (A) scolds him (B) nurses him back to health (C) sends him to St. Michael's (D) sells him to slave-traders.

DRAWING CONCLUSIONS

7 Betsy Freeland blames the escape plan on
   (A) her son (B) Sandy Jenkins (C) Douglass (D) William Hamilton.

8. After the fight at the shipyard, Master Hugh gets angry at
   (A) Mr. Gardner (B) the men who beat up Douglass (C) Douglass (D) himself.

USING YOUR REASON

9. Douglass's life was probably in danger at St. Michael's because the people thought he
   (A) was the leader of the escape attempt (B) struck a white man (C) was a thief (D) killed Demby.

10. If Douglass had been killed at the shipyard in the presence of 1,000 people, the killers probably
(A) would be hanged (B) would go free (C) would confess
(D) would have no defense.

THINKING IT OVER
1. The slaveholders suspect that Douglass led the escape attempt. From what you know about Douglass, why do you think they suspected him?
2. Douglass wasn't content when his life as a slave got better, but wanted freedom all the more. Why do you think that was?

Chapters 15–16, Appendix

FINDING THE MAIN IDEA
1. Chapter 15 is mostly about
(A) the details of Douglass's escape (B) the people who helped him escape (C) his trip North (D) the months leading up to his escape.
2. Chapter 16 is mostly about
(A) Douglass's first three years in the North (B) Douglass's return to the South (C) Douglass's role in government
(D) Douglass's children.
3. The Appendix is mostly Douglass's comments on
(A) valuations (B) the religion of slaveholders (C) freedom of speech (D) his friends in the North.

REMEMBERING DETAILS
4. After Master Thomas denies him permission to "hire his own time," Douglass
(A) quits working (B) becomes a house servant (C) asks permission from Master Hugh (D) gives up on the idea.
5. Master Thomas tells Douglass that he will
(A) take care of him (B) get him work in a shipyard (C) sell him in Georgia (D) put him in jail.
6. In New York, Douglass's motto is
(A) "Live free or die" (B) "In God we trust" (C) "Trust no man" (D) "Be prepared."

7. Douglass first begins to feel at ease as a public speaker at an anti-slavery convention in
   (A) Boston (B) New Bedford (C) Nantucket (D) New York.

DRAWING CONCLUSIONS
8. At the time Douglass wrote his book, the people who helped him escape probably
   (A) were dead (B) still lived in the South (C) went with him
   (D) didn't care if anyone knew they'd helped him.

9. Douglass changed his name
   (A) because his old one brought back bad memories
   (B) to be fashionable (C) so kidnappers wouldn't find him
   (D) he didn't like his old one.

USING YOUR REASON
10. One reason Douglass doesn't give details about his escape is
    (A) it would help slaveholders (B) they are too boring
    (C) he can't remember them (D) he was sworn to secrecy.

11. Douglass begins to read the *Liberator* because it
    (A) is a source of job openings (B) is the cheapest paper
    (C) is anti-slavery (D) comes out weekly.

THINKING IT OVER
1. When Douglass gave the money he'd earned to Hugh Auld, Auld sometimes gave part of it back. Was Douglass grateful? Explain why he felt the way he did.

2. How did the city and the people of New Bedford compare with Baltimore and its people? Give examples from the book. What did Douglass think about the prosperity in the North?